FINTRY

The Story and Memories of 180 Years of a Rural North-East School

Janet M Byth

Published in January, 2015

A catalogue record for this book is available from the British Library
ISBN 978-0-9570999-4-4

Design and typesetting by Leopard Press
LePress@btconnect.com

Printed and bound in Scotland

Published by Leopard Press
LePress@btconnect.com

Dedication

In Memory of my dear husband, Robert W Byth

And for the generations of pupils and teachers
who knew Fintry School

Contents

Contributors

Maggie Mitchell (*née* Chapman)
Caroline Leggat
Kathleen McGowan
Frances Towler (Leggat)
James Cheyne
William Will
Agnes Bolwell (Gibson)
M Coreena Stephen (Cowie)
W Murray Ledingham
Lilias McKenzie (Cruickshank)
Ethel McCurrach (Cruickshank)
Sheila Morrison (Cruickshank)
Jean Skene (McBain)
Cathella Mitchell (Anderson)
Maisie Cheyne (Macdonald)
Myra Simmers (Leggat)
Janet Byth (Glennie)
John Glennie
Evelyn Strachan (Adam)
Maxwell Glennie
John Ledingham
Kathleen Reid (Anderson)
George and Jean Norrie
Alexander Norrie
Andrew Norrie
Catriona Tawse
Richard Stafford
Alfie Cheyne
Louise Grieve (Benzie)
Helen Findlay
Sheila McHattie
Jan Filshie
Jane Mack and teachers and parents 2011-13
Primary 7 pupils 2011-12

Acknowledgments

Many people and institutions have helped in the formation of this book, and heartfelt thanks are due to all of them. They include **Professor Ian Russell, Dr David Northcroft,** and all staff at the Elphinstone Institute; the staff of **Sir Duncan Rice Library** and **Special Collections and Archives,** University of Aberdeen; **Ruaridh Wishart** and the staff of Aberdeen City Archives; **Aberdeen Central Library** and **Aberdeenshire Library and Information Services,** Oldmeldrum; the **National Archives of Scotland,** Charlotte Square, Edinburgh, for Kirk Session and High Court records; **Aberdeenshire Council,** for the block plan of the school and the map of the school's catchment area; the **National Library of Scotland,** for the 1826 John Thomson map of the Fintry area, and **Turriff and District Heritage Society; Maisie Cheyne,** who set me on this project and my brother **Duncan Glennie** for help with photographs.

I am grateful to **Ian Hamilton** and **Lindy Cheyne** of Leopard Press for their interest, support and expertise in the editing and publishing of this work.

On a personal note, my family deserve sincere thanks for their loving encouragement, especially my three granddaughters, **Lily, Robyn** and **Carrie,** for providing light relief.

Without the enthusiastic and willing support of everyone at Fintry, this project would not have come to fruition. They are: **Ms Jane Mack, Mrs Una Ogg,** and all the staff and pupils at Fintry School; **John Ledingham** and **George and Jean Norrie** for access to privately owned documents, and all the former pupils, teachers, parents and community members who have so graciously shared their precious memories and photographs of schooldays.

Foreword

Fintry School is a fairly typical rural school of the North-East of Scotland. For more than 180 years, it has provided education for its community near Turriff, Aberdeenshire. The name, Fintry, comes from the Gaelic for 'a pleasant place by the side of a stream', and you may judge for yourself whether it would have been pleasant or otherwise for those generations of schoolchildren.

From Jessie Barclay's 'wrist swollen both morn and afternoon' in 1885, through Maisie's 1940s 'ruler over the knuckles', to today's enjoyment in learning, Fintry's story reflects North-East children's experience of rural education. Wherever you attended school, I hope this may resonate with your own experience, and if you or your ancestors attended Fintry, I trust the events, the teachers and the pupils described here provide some happy memories for you.

The first 30 years

The school appears to have been founded in 1831. The minutes of its 1859 committee of management says that the site was allocated for the school by the Earl of Fife in 1830. The accounts of King Edward kirk session note an annual donation of £1 to the *'school at Slap'* from 1831 until 1846, then a grant to the *'school of Fintry'* in 1861. (Slap is the old name for Fintry Farm)

Fintry was founded as a *'side'* school for the parishes of Turriff and King Edward, supported by subscription and a *'small sum'* from one of the heritors. By 1860, an annual subscription is also recorded which pays the schoolmaster's salary. The *New Statistical Account* (1840s) for Turriff implies that Fintry provided more than the elementary education offered at schools at Hatton and Gask.

At the 1841 census, a teacher named James Wilson, aged 19, lived at Slap with the Murray family, and 10 years later, Hector Black, unmarried, 33, a teacher of English born at Old Deer, occupied the Schoolhouse at Slap. The fact that the earliest known probable teacher at Fintry lived with the Murray household may indicate that William Murray, a *'very skilful practical farmer in this parish,'* was one of the main supporters of the school. (His daughter Anne married John Ledingham, and he and their descendants have played a significant role in the subsequent history of the school)

Education Provision in the 1830s

An Act of Parliament of 1803 encouraged the building of new schools, stipulating that a schoolhouse and a garden of at least ¼ acre Scots be provided for each parish school. The standard model was a rectangular two-storey building with the schoolroom below the master's two-roomed dwelling. From 1839 the Privy Council Committee on Education in London offered grants for maintenance as well as building, and encouraged some training for teachers.

A table of school fees was to be displayed in every schoolroom, and the master was obliged to teach free any poor children of the parish entrusted to him. Every parish schoolmaster was examined and approved by the local presbytery, and had to sign the Confession of Faith and the Formula of the Church of Scotland. The act also provided for additional or 'side' schools where there was a need in a parish; these could be supported by public subscription and fees charged for each subject taught.

A new building

A petition in 1859 to the Earl of Fife from the local people reminded him of his promise to grant a deed in perpetuity on the site and garden of the school, and also to give £4 per annum towards the schoolmaster's salary. In response, the earl asked the petitioners to nominate trustees in whom to vest the property, and a meeting called on 13 April 1859 at the school was attended by 14 local people:

Alexander Ledingham, Barnyards of Delgaty, elder of Turriff kirk session; George Barclay, Yonderton, elder of King Edward kirk session; William Morrison, Upper Cotburn; George Ironside, Mill of Fintry; John Ledingham, Slap; William Hay, Ferniestripe; John Smart, Craigston; Robert Hay, blacksmith, Slap; ? Duncan, Plaidy; Lewis Wilson, blacksmith, Craigston; George Morrison, Millseat; John Paterson, Whinpark; ? Ingram, Walkerhill; and William Robb, schoolmaster.

George Barclay was appointed Chairman of the meeting, and several resolutions were carried:

A. *that the Kirk Sessions of Turriff and King Edward be nominated Trustees of the property with power to nominate or appoint a local Committee of Management,*

B. *that John Ledingham, Slap, be Secretary to carry on the correspondence to negotiate government aid to make the necessary addition to the building and augment the teacher's salary,*

C. *that George Barclay be appointed Treasurer to receive all contributions and open and manage a deposit account with the Union Bank, Turriff, in the name of Fintry School Committee,*

D. *that the Management Committee would confer with the Kirk Sessions on the best means of raising the salary and monies for the building, and*

E. *that Minutes and Accounts be kept.*

James Wood, Midtown, ? Goldsman, Milltown of Craigston, George Wilson, Badentyre and other local annual subscribers were also to be part of the committee.

The kirk session and minister of the parish of Turriff in which the school was situated were the lawful trustees, but because many of the scholars at Fintry came from King Edward and Monquhitter parishes, the London Committee

▶ **Fintry area** in 1832, John Thomson's map

Troup Head
Knock Head
Blackpots Brickwork & Harb.
Boyndie River
Dovern River
Cale Rock
Mellrose Head
Gamrie Head
Gardenstown Harbour
Pennan Head
Pennan Farm
Millstone Quarry
Northfield
Crovie
Old Castle
Stonewall
Knowhead
Lichnet
Protstown
Newtack
Glenquithel
Mains of Auchmedden
Newfarm
Chapelden
Pittyvaddar
Aberdour
Lemna
Foresterhill
Ardlawhill
Helenmore
Glenhouse
Windyheads
Cowford
BANFF
MACDUFF
Gallowhill
Woodside
Mill of Cullen
Mellrose
Mill of Mellrose
Cullen
Newton
Silverforth
Cross Butts
Greenstairs
Findon
Dubford
Myresss
Boghead
Bauds
Whitestones
Langman Hill
Jackstown
Birkenbauds
Mountbleaton Quarry
Hungryhills
Invericharny
Keelhill
Foulzie
Over Foulzie
Eden Cottage
Fortry
Mill of Fortry
Balgreen
Ruins of Eden Castle
Mill of Eden
Mill of Pitgerr
Cummertown
Clochforbie
Braes
Faughfolds
Milltown
Mains of Fishery
Mill of Fishery
Auchlin
Blakesbog
Crudie
Little Byth
Bracklamore
Todpole
Ballmaad
Walkerhill
Castletown
Ruins of a Castle
Strathapple
Cowbog
Blackburn
Pitsligo Hill
Cairnywhing
Tillanamont
Muttonbrae
Ruins of Allyah
Mountblairy
Mill of Mountblairy
Burreldales
Commissarybog
Maryhill
Mountblairy House
Brownside
Crannabog
Boghead
Auchmill
Gardneystown
Craigston Castle
Fintry
Slackadale
Lucarty
Fairystrype
Litterty
Tillymauld
NEW BYTH
Newtonhead
Headitown
Bonnykelly
Boat of Skogie
L. Haughs
Haughs
Kinminty
Crossfield
Brackans
Burnside
Barnyards
Cairnhill
Greystone
Garmond Vill
Millfield House
Auchry House
Middlethird
Belthangies
Whitestone
Whitecairns
Old Whitl
Broomhill
Ironsides
Knockiemill
Meadowheads
Delgaty House
Mill of Turriff
TURRIFF
Castletown
Inchar
Hair moss
CUMINESTON
Woodhead
Crosshill
Wolfhill
Bye Rush
Fedderat Castle
Scobach
FORGLEN
Forglen House
Crookwell
Carnousie House
Carnousie Cottage
Oldtown
Cranna
Skabhill
Cluny House
Brokentobill
Sandlaw
Dallachy
Dallachies
Denhead
Montcoffer
Muirside
Newton
Mounderlea
Duchaross
Whitefield
Skaterie Holm
Holy Mill
Balchers
Muirtown
Monkshill
Mains of Fishery

on Education accepted that three others, the Rev. William Findlay, minister of King Edward, and George Barclay and John Ledingham, join them as managers.

The school had *'always been described as an established Kirk of Scotland school'* and this was continued. The bond was signed in March 1861 in both parishes; it assigned ownership to the trustees, *'for a school… for the children of labouring, manufacturing and the poorer classes and for a residence for the teacher or teachers'*.

The first managers were the Rev. John Cruickshank (Turriff), the Rev. William Findlay (King Edward), John Hannay (factor for the Earl of Fife), John Rose (factor for Mr Urquhart of Craigston), Alexander Ledingham (Barnyards), George Barclay (Yonderton), William Morrison (Lower Cotburn), William Morrison (Upper Cotburn) and John Ledingham (Slap). The committee was elected from subscribers who gave ten shillings (50p) annually, with those giving five shillings being eligible to vote.

Plans were made to extend the existing building, but as these did not meet with Committee on Education regulations, James Duncan, architect, Turriff, was asked to draw up plans and prepare estimate specifications for a new school. The managers suggested an asphalt floor, but the reply came: *'My lords cannot possibly sanction an asphalt floor for the schoolroom. It is probably the very worst kind of floor for such a purpose'*.

Decisions had to be made whether to use white Baltic or red Norway pine for the flooring, and wooden pegs or cast-iron fixings, and questions answered about the effect on the school of the line of the new road from the Turriff-Banff turnpike to Craigston Castle.

Contractors were then appointed at these quoted prices:

James Massie, mason	£59.5.0
George Lovie, rubble quarrier	(blank)
John Smart, carpenter	£63.10.0
William Anderson, slater	£18.0.0
I. Gibson, plasterer	£8.10.0
I. Robison, excavator	(blank)

The plan of 1861 shows a one-roomed building, a

▶ **The 1861 school plan** showing the original schoolhouse

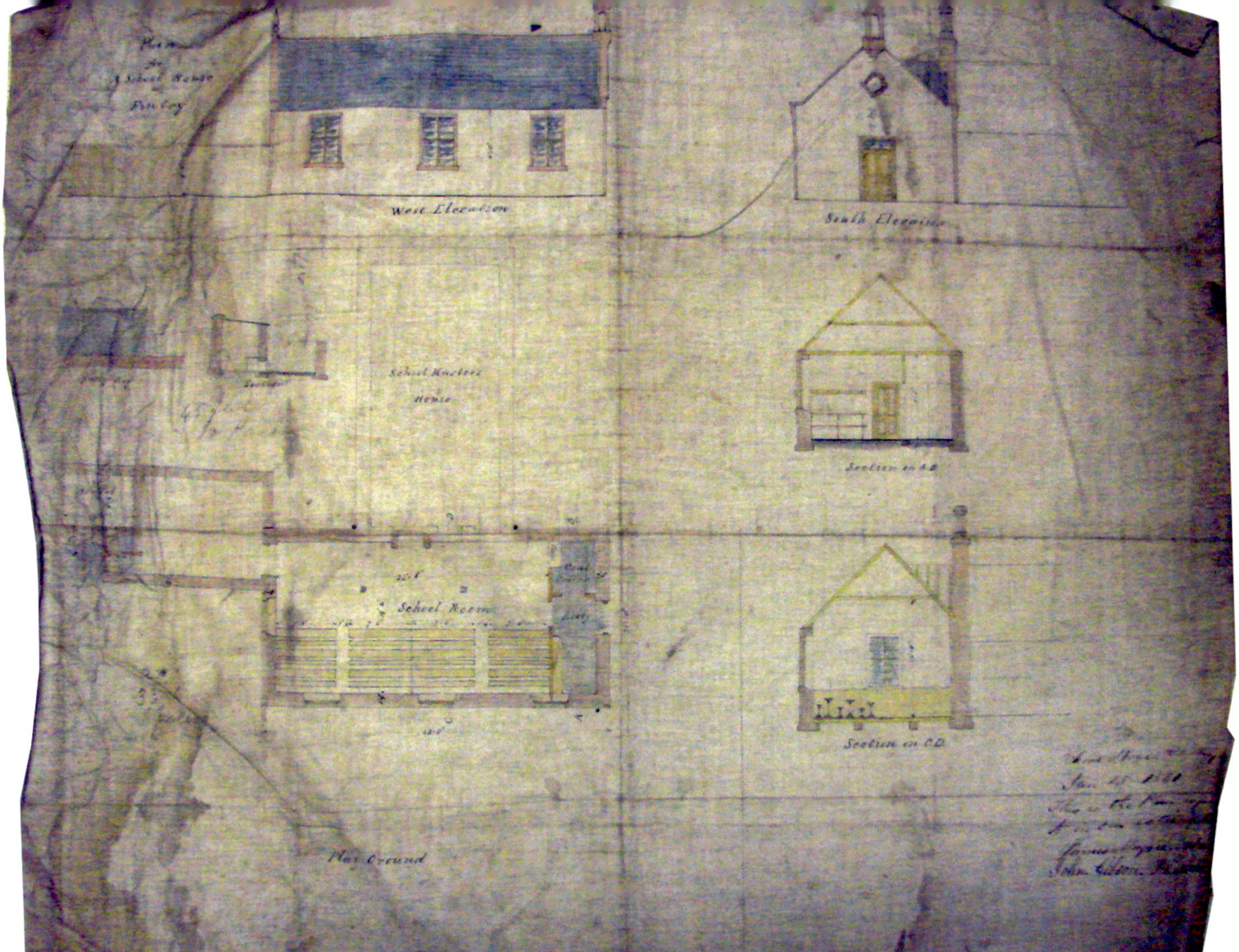
West Elevation
South Elevation
School Master's House
School Room
Section on A.B
Section on C.D
Play Ground

schoolroom of 35 feet 6 inches long, with three rows of benches and desks along its length, facing a fireplace against the wall adjoining the schoolmaster's dwelling (the original school). On the north end, a door led out to the privies and the ash pit. A playground lay to the west, surrounded by a boundary wall. The land allowed a garden and enough land on the north side for the master to *'keep a cow'*. The school was completed that year, with best Baltic timber floors after all.

The subscribers

The subscriptions raised in 1859 from collections in Turriff and King Edward churches were short by £16.13.0, even after Mr Urquhart of Craigston gave £15.15.0 to pay for roofing timber and £2 per annum towards the master's salary, but in October 1860 the annual collection raised some more money for building and to pay Mr Robb, the schoolmaster. The Committee on Education awarded a grant of £123 towards the cost of building and furnishing. The balance was found by using funds donated by friends *'at a distance'* and intended for the dwelling-house, and by a second assessment of the managers. *(See APPENDIX 1: Abstract of Subscription Lists and Disbursements 1859–1862)*

Masters and assistants

William Robb, schoolmaster, died aged 30 of consumption, before the new school was built. According to John Ledingham this was 'apparently hastened if not originated by confinement in too small apartments'. *(See APPENDIX 2: Timeline of Fintry School Head Teachers)*

His successor, William Hay, came to Fintry with certificates of good moral character from several of the professors of King's College. He also had a certificate from the parish of Old Deer testifying to his energy and success while assistant teacher at Clochcan School.

When the two parish ministers inspected the school in March 1862, his resignation was accepted on grounds of ill-health. The assistant, George Anderson had been praised for his work by the inspecting ministers, and Turriff Kirk Session approved the trustees' choice of him as schoolmaster. When the first government inspection of Fintry took place in early 1865 he had gained a third class, third division Certificate of Merit in teaching. By 1866 there was a sewing mistress, Jane Hay, working in addition to the master.

On Anderson's resignation to become schoolmaster at Udny Parish School, the school managers noted with regret 'the loss of a good teacher'. With the assistant, James Paterson, as interim teacher, the managers asked Her Majesty's Inspector (HMI) Black to recommend a successor. John Arnott was a certificated teacher, second class, division one. He was 24 years old and married, and his wife Isabella soon started work, unpaid, as the industrial teacher, giving sewing and knitting lessons to the girls.

When Helen Wilson was examined by HMI for suitability as a pupil teacher, there were 95 scholars on the roll, 60 boys and 35 girls.

Her appointment would have raised the proportion of teachers to scholars above the legal minimum, and the managers were reminded by the inspectorate that they were responsible for paying their teachers without any support other than the government grant.

Pupil teachers received a small salary and free education for five years in return for assisting the teacher. Applicants had to be 13 years of age, healthy, able to read fluently and write neatly. They had to sit an exam in spelling and punctuation, do sums in the four elementary rules, point out simple parts of speech and understand elementary geography: religious knowledge had to be sound, girls had to be able to knit and sew, and all had to teach a junior scholar to HMI's satisfaction. The teacher was paid for training them. Not more than one pupil teacher could be employed for every 25 scholars.

The managers replied that they failed *'to see the force* [of the above] *as a valid objection, as the person to whom Helen Wilson is to be apprenticed is only the industrial assistant and wife of the certificated master and not receiving pay and no special number of scholars can be assigned to her'*. In November the Committee on Education declined her as a pupil teacher *'except the teaching of industrial work be teaching* (sic) *all day'*.

John Arnott's successor, Alexander Stephen, had a younger brother, Robert, who started work as a pupil teacher, and in April 1871 James Morrison, son of the grocer at Craigston, was registered as a pupil teacher, with 122 scholars on the roll.

Fees

The application in October 1862 for a government grant shows that there were no children classified as infants (under six years of age) in the school at that time.

Rates of weekly payment, and numbers of children paying at each rate *(Annual Grants Form, ED/18, National Archives of Scotland):*

RATES IN PENCE	2½	3	3½	4
Boys	17	9	8	5
Girls	7	6	4	4
Infants	0	0	0	0

The rate of fee rose with the number of subjects taken. The authorities wanted fees to be dependent on either *'the means of the parents or according as a child passes from the lower to the higher classes in a school. The highest class in a school should be accessible for a fee fairly within the means of a common labouring man in the neighbourhood.'*

The school year

The summer vacation normally stretched from the end of August, or the beginning of September, to October or November, once the harvest was in. In 1870, with fever rife in the district, school closed early on 15 July; it reopened only on 15 September, and the fever epidemic lingered on until mid-October.

Scholars usually returned gradually after holiday periods and attendance increased towards the end of the school terms. Epidemics of measles, diphtheria, *'the Itch'* (an eruptive skin disease caused by a parasitic mite), influenza, whooping-cough, scarletina and scarlet fever (and even typhoid fever in one family in May 1872) ensured that numbers were often very low. Occasionally children were kept at home on the rumour of an epidemic. The school was closed for almost a week in May 1865 for thorough cleaning after a diphtheria outbreak.

Helping with sowing, turnip-hoeing, herding, cutting peat, harvesting, and potato-lifting kept attendances irregular for the boys: girls were called on to look after younger siblings while mothers worked in the fields, or to help with the cleaning before the family moved. Farm servants frequently moved after the feeing markets, so that many children attended several schools in their childhood.

There was an annual school holiday for the harvest thanksgiving in November, then the Martinmas feeing markets could mean an influx of new children to complicate the master's teaching programme. Lack of daylight caused school hours to be cut short from November until February (9.30AM to 3.30PM instead of 9AM to 4PM).

John Arnott wrote in the log book on 1 January 1869 that *'the children were quite overjoyed, and were quite enthusiast* (sic) *in wishing the master a Happy New Year'*. After a holiday from 4 to 8 January, *'the master and parents treated the children to a splendid Christmas Tree on 11 January* (Auld Yule). *Drawing tickets for gifts commenced at 1PM and ended about 4.30 PM. A great many parents and friends turned out to see the sight: and the children enjoyed themselves thoroughly.'*

Alexander Stephen noted on 25 December 1871, a school day as normal, that *'the people in this district are so conservative as to prefer Auld Yule'* to Christmas. January to March was usually noted for low attendances because of bad weather and illness, but Her Majesty's Inspector called at some point during those months for the annual inspection. There was much preparation of the scholars for this visit.

On Shrove Tuesday, also called Fastern's Eve or Brose Day, the children sometimes had an early finish or a half-holiday; then the emphasis was on learning the Shorter Catechism in time for the minister's examination. The fast day holidays, of three or four days before communion services in the parish church, took place soon afterwards. As Fintry was on the borders of two parishes, the Turriff and King Edward scholars were sometimes absent at different times for their fast days.

The presbytery inspection and a meeting of the school's managers meant a few hours off for the children, and Whitsunday at the end of May meant more changes as families moved farms.

At the Lammas Fair in late July, scholars went to Turriff for the engaging of hands for the harvest. Turriff cattle show in early August was often an excuse for absence, as were local holidays for Plaidy, Millseat and Craigston. A school excursion to Fyvie took place in August 1867. The following year, the school went farther afield, to Inverurie and Keith-hall.

The end of August brought examinations, and while there is no record of where the money came from for prizes, there was some fund-raising; on 26 November 1866 a *soirée* was held under the auspices of the Temperance Society and the children were treated the next day to the left-over tea and biscuits.

On 10 May 1869 Mr Stewart, second master in Milne's Institution, Fochabers, visited. A colporteur (a pedlar selling religious tracts and books) called in October 1868, and the master, John Arnott, bought books *'to distribute among the most diligent scholars, as a means of encouragement'*. Mr Love gave an afternoon lecture to the scholars on 21 December 1870 on the subject of the Holy Land, and the school had a holiday for the wedding of Princess Louise and the Marquis of Lorne on 21 March 1871. On 3 July 1872 a photographer from Turriff came to take a group photograph of the scholars, the first time in the school's history.

There were sad occasions too. John Arnott was called away on 6 May 1867 as his brother *'was at the point of death'* and James Morrison, pupil teacher, was absent on 29 January 1872 *'on account of his sister's death'*, reminders of the high death toll among younger people in Victorian times.

Curriculum and textbooks

The school's Feu Charter of 1861 stipulated that reading, writing, arithmetic, geography, scripture and history be taught, with needlework for girls and Bible reading daily, but learning the catechism was to be dependent on the wishes of the parents.

When George Anderson began to keep the log book in February 1864, reading, writing, arithmetic, geography, history and Bible Knowledge were all taught. A Latin class was formed in April, taking place half-an-hour before regular school hours.

Under John Arnott, homework, previously given weekly, was nightly; grammar and geography were taught on alternate days, mental arithmetic was tested after 4PM – those who answered quickest getting away first. Arithmetic and map drawing were done on slates, but writing to dictation in copybooks. Newspapers instead of reading books were read on Mondays by the two highest classes and a second Latin class was started.

One scholar who wished to be a banker's clerk was taught book-keeping. Mrs Arnott taught sewing to the girls, who brought their '*seams*' from home.

Much of the curriculum was to our eyes very academic for pupils aged from six to thirteen years. English and grammar included the etymology of words and analysis of sentences; history covered the pre-Norman period to the foreign policy of Oliver Cromwell. Geography taught the ancient, medieval and modern world, Asia and Africa, Palestine and Ireland, and Bible examinations were on the Old Testament books of Joshua, Judges, Ruth and the prophets.

The textbooks used were *CONSTABLE'S READING BOOKS*, *STEP BY STEP* and *SEQUEL TO STEP BY STEP*, and *COLLIER'S BRITISH HISTORY*. The children were *'highly delighted'* with the practice of drawing on the slate from a pattern on the blackboard.

In February 1867 Helen Wilson, started teaching singing, then Alexander Stephen introduced singing to a scale written on the blackboard, *'and the children showed that they were not altogether ignorant of the subject.'*

He found that the children's knowledge of the meaning of words was below standard and introduced *MORRELL'S GRAMMAR*. He taught *'profit and loss'*, and had a Latin class comprised largely of girls. At times he comments that school is noisy because of arithmetic being repeated aloud. In November 1870, a story was read to the two higher classes, *'the substance of it to be told by them as an exercise in composition.'*

Examinations, inspections and prizes

Every year the minister of Turriff Parish Church, the Rev. John Cruickshank, examined the pupils on the catechism. Because the Church of Scotland did not want to give up its control of education, their reports have to be read with caution. The Rev. Cruickshank and Rev. Findlay pronounced teaching at Fintry to be satisfactory in all branches in 1863, and this opinion prevailed to the last presbytery visit in May 1873.

More objective reports come from the government inspection. In 1867, inspector John Black said, *'The work is carefully done, and the number of passes creditable; but a larger number should have been entered for individual examination. The new master* (John Arnott) *promises well'*.

Payment of the grant in full was recommended to augment the master's salary, but if more pupils had been examined and failed, the grant would have been reduced under the *'payment by results'* regime.

The HMI reports refer to very good discipline in the school, and to the children being encouraged by rewards and prizes.

Upgrading

The committee set up in 1861 managed the school until 1873. The Rev. William Findlay, George Barclay, Yonderton and John Ledingham, Slap were re-elected every May until 1869 when the Rev. Donald Stewart, assistant minister at King Edward, replaced William Findlay who *'had for 40 years taken an active interest in the school'* but was now in failing health.

The managers and the community voted unanimously in 1867 to have the school raised to the status of a second parochial school, and made plans for improving the master's dwelling and altering the school building to conform to the regulations of the Board of Education.

With the Rev. Stewart chairing a sub-committee of George Barclay (Yonderton), Robert Gibbon (Brackens), Peter Cowie (Kinminty), George Barclay (Mains of Craigston), George Ironside (Mill of Fintry), Peter Gaul (Whiterashes) and John Ledingham (Slap), and £40.4.10d subscribed, it was resolved to proceed with the plans drawn up by James Duncan, and hold a bazaar in Turriff to help with costs. This took place in August 1872, organised by three of the local farmers under the patronage of Mrs Pollard Urquhart of Craigston and manned by the farmers' wives and daughters, assisted by some ladies from beyond the area. *(See APPENDIX 3: Account of Receipts and Expenditure in Connection with the Schoolmaster's House and Porch.)*

School and community

The Fintry branch of the Ploughman's Mutual Improvement Association (MIA) was set up in the mid-1860s, the first adult organisation to meet in the school. Occasional lectures were held in the school, such as one given by an American freed slave in January 1868.

▶ **Bazaar:** Banffshire Journal, 13 August 1872

BAZAAR AT TURRIFF.

A BAZAAR in aid of the fund for the liquidation of the debt on the schoolmaster's house at Fintry, parish of Turriff, was held in Turriff on Tuesday last in a handsome and spacious marquee. Some time ago the schoolhouse got into a very dilapidated condition, so much so that it was absolutely necessary that extensive repairs should be made upon it. There were no available funds, however, for this purpose, and some friends in the locality subscribed handsomely and liberally. But the amount raised in this manner proved inadequate; for a further sum of nearly £80 was required. Three gentlemen—Mr Barclay, Yonderton; Mr Cowie, Kinminty; and Mr Gibbon, Brackens—kindly guaranteed this amount. It was for the laudable purpose of having this debt cleared off that the bazaar was held.

The school of Fintry is an incalculable boon to those in the locality, which may be judged from the fact that over 130 pupils is the average attendance; and the school is about four miles from any other. This circumstance, along with the respect in which the teacher, Mr Stephen, is held, made it the more to be hoped that the friends of education would come forward and give their utmost support to forward the scheme. Nor were those interested disappointed. Ample time was given to the influential Committee of ladies, with Mrs Pollard Urquhart of Craigston as Lady Patroness, to prepare and collect from friends the necessary miscellanies for the occasion. The result of their efforts, when viewed on Tuesday, bore ample proof of the exertions they had made, and the time spent in the cause. The bazaar was opened at eleven o'clock forenoon by the Rev. John Cruickshank, D.D., of the Manse, who said:—

Ladies and gentlemen,—The ceremony of opening the Bazaar having devolved upon me, I am glad to think that only a few words of explanation can be needed, with a view to secure its object. It has been got up—you see with what beautiful effect—as the best mode of obtaining the means to liquidate a debt pressing somewhat injuriously on the interests of education at Fintry. The school there is unendowed. The erection of the buildings, and the support of the master, have for many past years fallen as a burden chiefly on the inhabitants of the district. They have done their part liberally and well. But lately, finding it necessary to expend a considerable sum of money in providing suitable accommodation for a teacher, whose usefulness they appreciate, and whose services they are most anxious to retain, they look now to their friends to assist them in placing pecuniary matters on a better footing than they are. The sale of the varied, valuable, and beautiful work exhibited in the Bazaar will accomplish this object, and extinguish the present debt. And besides, the success of this undertaking will amply reward the ladies presiding over the stalls for their kind and beneficent exertions. I now declare the Bazaar opened, with hearty good wishes for its success.

The airiness and roominess of the marquee made it admirably suited for the accommodation of the stalls, of which there were four. The general arrangement of these, combined with the neat, handsome, and various coloured articles, displayed to catch both eye and purse, presented quite a gay appearance.

We may shortly mention a few of the contents of the stalls, without even attempting to do them full justice, for, in fact, it would prove an utter impossibility.

The centre one, facing you as you entered, was presided over by Mrs Dr Cruickshank of the Manse; Mrs Milne, King-Edward; Mrs Morrison, Auchlin, and Mrs Bartlett, Easter Bo. They were assisted by the Misses Cruickshank of the Manse; Miss Morrison, Auchlin; Misses Milne, Newburgh, Fifeshire; and Miss Smith, Aberdeen. On this tastefully laid out stall there was some good drawings in chalk and water colours. A noticeable article was a handsome rug, apparently wrought from useless cuttings of cloth, now utilised and formed into a tasteful design. There were also some very fine pieces of sewed work, which must have cost the zealous hands a deal of care. A bed-cover, in squares, with scriptural texts, being quite original, was much admired. These, with a host of other wares, such as tidies, antimacassars, cushions, mats, slippers, &c., &c., were all in tempting array.

The stand on the right was presided over by Mrs Barclay, Yonderton; and Mrs Morrison, Balmellie Street, who were assisted by the Misses Morrison, Balmellie Street; and the Misses Mitchell, Balgreen. To a certain extent, the display on this stand was not unlike that of the former. The article that claimed pre-eminence was a group of three figures (in miniature) representing, as we were informed by a card attached, 'A scene in Kensington Gardens in the reign of George II.' The trio comprised a lady dressed in very antique costume, with a black slave in attendance, and lamb in background. The brocade of the dress, we were further informed, 'was worn by a member of the Earl of Aberdeen's family 130 years ago.'

We may mention that this trio of contrasts realized £3 5s.

The worsted winder or wince, in varnished pine, was both handsome and useful.

The stall on the left was presided over by Mrs Gibbon, Brackens; Mrs Cowie, Kinminty; and Mrs Hutcheon, Lower Cotburn; who were assisted by Misses Barnett, Kirkton, Fraserburgh; Misses Hutcheon, Victoria Terrace; Misses Macdonald, Kindrought; Miss Allan, teacher, Turriff; Misses Cowie, Kinminty; and the Misses Gibbon, Brackens. The taste displayed on the other stalls was not awanting here, and a varied assortment of ornamental sewed work, children's dresses, and other useful knicknacks, and some good stands of croquet essentials found ready purchasers.

The Refreshment Stall, apart from the others, was presided over by Mrs Morrison, Upper Cotburn, assisted by Miss Morrison, and Miss Barclay, Yonderton. It had its full quota of customers. The General Post-Office was conveniently situated—Mr Barclay, North of Scotland Bank, ably officiating as post-master-general for the day; and, by his financial budget, we may judge he was worthy of the confidence reposed in him.

The lottery tub was profitably conducted by a band of little ladies and gentlemen, viz.—Miss Jeanie Morrison, Balmellie Street; Miss Maggie Barclay, Yonderton; Master Gibbon, Brackens; and Master Barclay, Yonderton.

That respectable old lady, whose memory is ever associated with her peculiar voracious mania for clay pipes, was taken care of by Mr Stephen, teacher, Fintry; and it is only meet that we mention those gentlemen who took charge of the entrance, and discharged the onerous duties of attending—namely, Mr Cowie, Kinminty, and Mr Gibbon, Brackens.

Large numbers patronised the bazaar throughout the day, the majority, we are glad to say, being of the number of those

'Whose hearts the tide of kindness warms
Who hold their being on the terms,
Each aid the others.'

And thus, instead of victims being snared, we are sure that purchases were willingly made, all being anxious that the result should be successful, and we are requested to state that even Mr John Williamson, Turriff, willingly added his quota by posting the bills, &c., gratis.

The sale continued untiringly up to about seven o'clock evening, and, during the whole long day, the unflagging zeal of the ladies at their self-imposed duties was unremitting.

After this hour, the few minor articles remaining undisposed of were sold by auction, of which we now give a statement.

The proceeds are, we are glad to say, much over in amount the most sanguine expectations:—

	£	s	d
Centre Stand, ...	£32	16	10
Right Hand Stand, ...	46	5	9
Left Hand Stand, ...	38	8	11
Refreshment Stand, ...	5	1	0
Admission Money, ...	13	10	0
Aunt Sally, ...	2	9	4
Post Office, ...	1	8	1
Lottery Tub, ...	1	4	11
Making the grand total of	£141	4	10

It will be observed that this handsome amount more than covers the debt. And we are informed that the available balance will be expended in erecting a porch in front, and in enlarging the schoolroom, which, at present, is rather small for the large attendance.

A string band played at intervals throughout the day.

We may give our testimony to the good arrangements in the conducting of the bazaar; and we should add that it was greatly owing to the exertions of Mr Barclay, Yondertown, that the arrangements were so satisfactorily carried out.

Turriff school board – the first years

'A terrible row in Turra'

On 20 January 1873, the Rev. WP Smith, a prominent Free Church minister, gave a lecture in Turriff on the significance of the Education Act. He spoke of the extensive powers and influence invested in the new school boards and hence the importance of choosing good independent men.

A lively and good-humoured meeting of about 300 ratepayers was held in the town hall under the chairmanship of Baillie Hutcheon. He expressed the view that *'the man possessed with good common sense and a fair elementary education is… as well qualified to be a member of the school board as if he had been a professor of Greek, Hebrew, Latin, of Mathematics or of Chemistry'*.

It was decided that there would be a free and open election in Turriff - *'a*

The Education (Scotland) Act 1872

A Board of Education, later the Scotch Education Department (SED), was established in Edinburgh.

Every parish had its School Board responsible for all the schools in the parish. These boards, elected by property owners and occupiers worth £4 annually, managed the school fund, kept the buildings in order, employed teachers, ensured attendance and received the reports of HMI. Parliamentary grants, the local 'school rate' and the fees paid by the parents made up the school fund. If fees were beyond the means of a parent, the parochial board paid them.

All teachers in office when the Act was passed stayed in post. Every teacher had to have a Certificate of Competency. HMI could recommend dismissal of incompetent teachers, but a sheriff had to deal with 'immoral conduct or cruel or improper treatment' of scholars.

Attendance was compulsory to the age of 13 by 1878. If a child under thirteen was employed, the employer and the parents had to see that the child attended evening continuation classes, or a certificate of exemption could be granted if the child had reached a set standard. School board officers were appointed to check and report reasons for absence. HMI inspected every school annually, and Parliamentary grants were awarded or curtailed on the recommendation of the inspectors.

Religious instruction was allowed as part of the curriculum, at the beginning or the end of the school day, a 'conscience clause' for parents who might wish to remove their children from the subject.

terrible row in Turra', said the Baillie. Candidates were heckled. The main topics of interest were their independence from landowners and the balance of fees and rates – most candidates wanted fees kept easily within the reach of parents.

At the election on 12 April, the successful candidates were:

Member	Occupation	Address	Denomination
John Hutcheon	Merchant	High Street	Established Church
James Grieve	Bank Agent	High Street	Established Church
Rev J. Sutherland	Clergyman	Free Manse	Free Church
Alexander Stuart	Proprietor	Laithers House	Established Church
John Ledingham	Farmer	Slap	Congregationalist
Patrick Cheyne	Merchant Tailor	Main Street	Episcopalian
George Bruce	Farmer	Little Hilton	Free Church

Alexander Stuart of Laithers was elected chairman of the board, his having had a liberal education at Aberdeen University, his assiduity in his public duties and his *'abundance of leisure'* recommending him for the task. Finance and school management committees were formed, with John Ledingham a member of the latter.

The board's census showed that the total number of children attending schools in the parish was 879 (433 males, 436 females). Of those, 110 (68 males, 42 females) attended Fintry. Only 61 of the Fintry pupils belonged to the parish of Turriff, with 23 from King Edward and 26 from New Byth. There were 20 children over the age of 13 in the school, and one under five, leaving 89 within the age-range for the new system.

Although daily Bible reading only had been the favoured choice of the candidates, the Rev. Sutherland fought a determined battle to have all the schools commence the day with prayer and three-quarters of an hour's religious instruction. With Messrs. Ledingham, Cheyne and Bruce dissenting, his motion was carried.

Fintry joins the system

In 1873 HMI John Kerr reported, *'I have again found this school very carefully and intelligently taught. The standard work is remarkably well done and the subjects beyond the standards continue to receive satisfactory attention'.*

Only 48 were present for this inspection on 5 March,

yet attendance was 101 for examination by the Rev. Donald Stewart on behalf of presbytery. The managers were re-elected *'until such time as the school may be transferred to the school board'* and the minister intimated that voluntary subscriptions to the schoolmaster's salary would lapse at the Whitsunday term.

On 17 June 1873, the last meeting of the trustees and managers took place. They were *'unanimously of the opinion that the school should be transferred to the school board of the parish'* on condition that the *'present teacher shall be retained in office, that his emoluments shall not be less than he has hitherto enjoyed; and that the provisions and conditions embodied in the charter granted by Lord Fife shall be observed'*. The transfer was completed by March 1874.

Changing teachers

Although Alexander Stephen's position was safeguarded by the Act, he resigned his appointment in January 1874 to go to Killearn public school in Stirlingshire. He seems to have been a popular and efficient teacher, but he had not been fully paid since the heritors' liability for salary had ended at Whitsunday 1873.

Robert Stephen, now 17, left his pupil-teachership soon after, and James Morrison completed his five-year apprenticeship the following January. He left after sitting the admission examination for the training college in Edinburgh. In April 1874 Miss McAndrew was appointed temporary industrial teacher of needlework.

The inspectors call

Inspector Smith's report of 1874 shows a *'comparatively large class had a sound knowledge of Latin'* and grammar, geography and composition were well taught. Of the 62 pupils presented for examination to the Inspector, 62 passed in reading, 60 in writing and 56 in arithmetic. A year later, under George Andrew, passes were down to 49 in reading, 56 in writing and 51 in arithmetic, and Inspector John Kerr found only two boys doing sound elementary Latin. He noted very good discipline, singing and industrial work in addition to good standard work and fair geography and history in the highest class, with only satisfactory standards in the lower classes. All these pupils were under the instruction of the master, a pupil-teacher and a part-time sewing teacher, and the master was also responsible for teaching the pupil-teachers Latin and some Greek. He also taught algebra to the oldest boys.

Outings

In 1873 the Banffshire Journal reported a juvenile excursion from Turriff, to Keith-Hall, the estate of the Earl of Kintore, by train. Two years later, the *'usual amusements'* were supplemented by *'object lessons'*, *'giving instruction and fun in happy combination; while the younger excursionists listened with attention to a graphic description of Jerusalem, given by a clergyman recently returned from the sacred city'*.

Petition

Early in 1875, a petition was presented to the board by 56 householders in the district. They alleged that, because Mr Andrew did not reside in the schoolhouse, the house and garden were deteriorating, and that the children were running wild in the morning and at midday, *'so much so that it is no uncommon thing to see them sitting astride the roof of the school near the belfry'*.

While Baillie Hutcheon thought that his non-residence made Mr Andrew inaccessible to the parents and guardians, the Rev. Sutherland thought nothing should be done harshly in dealing with the teacher whom he thought did his work well. John Ledingham did not think things were as bad as they were represented, as *'the schoolhouse was used daily for industrial teaching, and had a fire in one of the rooms every day'*. He thought *'the people who signed that petition were demoralising the district, for only fifteen children attended school both yesterday and today'*. Mr Andrew was offered and accepted a salary of £100 on condition he lived in the schoolhouse.

However, John Ledingham then visited the school, found numbers very low and concluded that *'there was neglect somewhere'*. The board officer reported that only 58 scholars attended Fintry, considerably fewer than there should have been. Mr Andrew left soon thereafter.

Room for expansion

An extra classroom was approved by the Scotch Board of

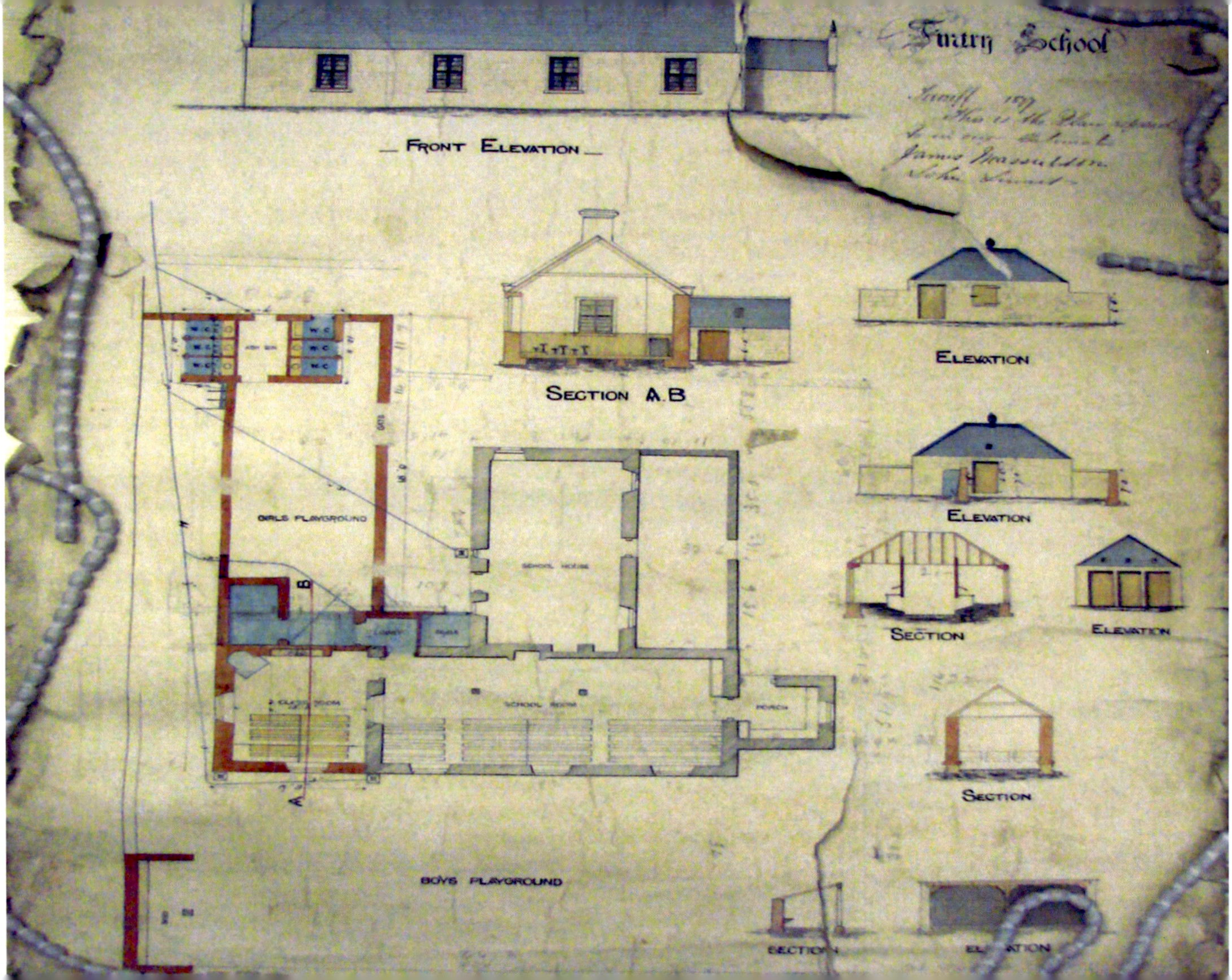

Fintry School
FRONT ELEVATION
SECTION A.B
ELEVATION
ELEVATION
SECTION
ELEVATION
SECTION
GIRLS PLAYGROUND
SCHOOL HOUSE
SCHOOL ROOM
PORCH
BOYS PLAYGROUND
SECTION
ELEVATION

Education in late 1876, and built over the following summer. The building was extended northwards, linking a smaller classroom to the existing one by a window and a door.

Baillie Hutcheon said that the aim was *'to have a classroom which the teacher could command at a glance, and still have a certain control over what was going on outside.'*

The materials specified matched the existing building and parts of the gable were re-used. Rows of seats and desks, with grooves for slates, matched the fittings in the original classroom, and a fireplace was built in the corner.

Troubled times

'A cool daring blackguard'

When Henry Boyd became schoolmaster, he had the advantage of having a wife who could carry out the industrial teaching. Boyd noted that the home lessons were *'very badly prepared ..., owing I suppose to the children being unaccustomed to get them... Some of those over seven cannot write a number of three figures – one boy does not know the figures.'*

He found his pupil teacher, John Scott, slow at his studies, and when the inspector visited in 1876, Scott had an unsatisfactory exam. *'Should he be required to complete the staff, and fail to the same extent next year, the grant will have to be reduced'*, warned Insp. Robert Harvey. John Scott left in October and was replaced by Isabella Wilson.

Boyd complained that his older pupils came only to make their 150 attendances and *'contribute their failures at the next examination'*, and that irregular attendees were *'a drag on the work of the school'*.

A boy was expelled for kicking the teacher and three candidates for pupil teachership refused to give assistance. The board rejected all three and advertised, and Joanna Adam was appointed in October 1881.

Isabella Wilson passed her pupil teacher exams in 1882 and brought a grant of £2 to the school. In addition to the two pupil teachers and Mrs Boyd, the school had a monitor, James Gaul, a senior pupil who was paid a small fee to help with teaching. The board officer, Sgt Nash, taught the boys military drill as well as checking on arrears of fees and irregular attendance.

Rumours were circulating about the schoolmaster's behaviour to the girls. William Morrison, the miller at Craigston, had two daughters who had become unwilling to attend school, and his wife eventually discovered the improper treatment they were suffering at Boyd's hands.

When John Hutcheon, farmer at Lower Cotburn, learned about the allegations, he asked the school board to act, but it only proposed that the parents take legal action. With no action forthcoming, John Hutcheon and John Ledingham made a formal complaint to the procurator-fiscal in Aberdeen.

On 19 January 1883, Boyd was arrested. He was examined in Aberdeen Sheriff Court before Sheriff Comrie

Thomson and *'committed for trial upon the charge of using lewd, indecent and libidinous practices and behaviour towards girls under 12 years of age; and also of shamelessly indecent conduct towards young girls at and about that age, aggravated by your being in the position of schoolmaster, and they being your scholars.'*

The fiscal considered that Boyd was *'a cool daring blackguard'* who had conducted himself indecently with every girl in the school *'who had occasion to stand or sit beside him'*. *'He still carries on the school though four-fifths of the scholars have left'*. He added that there was division in the district over Boyd, with a subscription being raised to help him defend himself. The fiscal also felt it was important that the trial be held as soon as possible, because the incessant talking about the case among the children of Fintry and neighbouring schools might affect the recollections of the witnesses.

At his trial, Boyd pleaded not guilty to charges of offences against four girls of around 11 years of age. Statements had been taken from them and from five other Fintry pupils, the police officer at Turriff, the mother of the Morrison girls and Joanna Adam, pupil teacher. There were three witnesses for Boyd, the Rev. James Sutherland, George Bruce, Little Hilton, and Henry Barclay, Craigston.

Evidence was led behind closed doors. When the jury returned after 22 minutes deliberation, they found Boyd guilty only of indecent behaviour. It was pointed out to them that they must return a verdict on the prisoner as charged, and after further deliberation, they brought in a guilty verdict. Lord Craighill, *'remarking that anything more scandalous than the prisoner's conduct he could hardly imagine,'* passed sentence of 18 months' imprisonment.

After serving his sentence, Boyd tried to sue the school board for his salary between his suspension and conviction, February-April 1883. Eventually the case was barred from proceeding further, and the board decided against any counter-claim for their expenses, as Boyd was *'beyond the jurisdiction of the Scotch courts'* and had *'little or no estate'*.

'Cruel and oppressive punishment'

William Charles Shand re-opened the school on 19 February 1883 with 80 pupils, pupil teacher Joanna Adam, interim industrial teacher Miss Cowie and monitor James Gaul.

The deferred inspection report was encouraging, the only criticism being of the industrial teaching. Miss Cowie (the farmer's daughter from Kinminty) was replaced by Miss Shand. When Miss Adam completed her apprenticeship and left for training college, James Gaul succeeded her, and Miss Williamina Paterson, Newton of Dunlugas, was appointed the first certificated assistant teacher in the school.

Charles Shand enjoyed cooperation at first, but soon the irregular attendees in the upper classes caused him problems; for example, Alex Morrison, *'who has always been troublesome'*, refused to hold out his hand for punishment for mistakes in his composition exercise.

Then Hugh Barclay, gardener at Craigston Castle, wrote to the board in July 1885 complaining of his daughter Jessie's treatment:

> *On 15th June her wrist was swollen both morn and afternoon. She was punished for not having sewing which was no fault of hers. Therefore I consider the punishment unlawful. She has knitting and canvas but not the specified sewing for next inspection, and I object to give her anything more until she has finished what she has begun. I strongly object to the principle of teaching children to lay aside work that is unfinished to begin new, it is unjust to parents as well as children. I wish it to be distinctly understood, that I do not object to any just or lawful punishment. But to the cruelty and oppression, that is carried on in Fintry School – I strongly object and protest against.*

Shand wrote in his defence to the board:

Hugh Barclay ...is, I understand, complaining about his girl being punished for not bringing sewing materials... to meet the requirements and satisfy HM Inspector. ..After the inspection (21 May), the girls were told what materials they would need for their new classes. Those who did not comply were repeatedly asked to do so without delay. This went on for three weeks, and on the afternoon of Mon. 15 June the girl in question, who, to make matters worse, was absent for four days of the previous week, one excuse being given to myself and another to officers, was punished (one smack on the hand) along with some others who then complied without more trouble. After being again absent for a fortnight less one day, she, Jessie Barclay, again returned without sewing when she was again warned without effect. On consideration and not being desirous of going to extremes, I have allowed her to attend school for fully three weeks without sewing, contrary to all discipline and the school arrange-

ments which is in itself an injustice to the rest of the pupils. This is only a repetition of former occasions, this family having been all along a source of very considerable annoyance, their general behaviour being of the rudest kind, and not only so, but their influence on the others has been anything but beneficial, not to speak of my own feelings and peace of mind, and I therefore consider their attendance at school against its best interests… It is needless to say that other disturbances, in school and out, have followed in the wake of the foregoing.

The board informed Barclay of Shand's denial of the charge and suggested that such charges *'are best disposed of by magistrates'*. They pointed out to him that parents must comply with the requirements of the Scotch Code (the national syllabus).

The schoolmaster again wrote to the board as Jessie Barclay still had not brought sewing materials to school by the end of term. The board replied that *'the parent must supply the material or withdraw the girl'*, and hoped that he would *'not compel the teacher to give effect to the order'*. There is no further reference to this matter, and Shand left Fintry in the following April.

'Rosy-cheeked lasses' and the 'sterner sex'

James Lawrence was a pupil at the school in the late 1870s, and his reminiscences in the *Banffshire Journal* provide a vivid picture of the district at this time. He was the eldest son of the cattleman at Upper Cotburn, who started his working life in the chaumer at Burnside of Delgaty, but went on to work in the armaments firm of Armstrong's on Tyneside.

SEE OVERLEAF ▶ **James Lawrence on Fintry School:**
Banffshire Journal, 10 October 1922

At the hill foot was the farm of Slap, and below that the Craigston Castle gardener's cottage, where lived then Mr Barclay, a refined gentlemanly person. A girl and boy attended school, both being of a nature less boisterous than most of us. The district owed much to Mr and Mrs Ledingham, for in good works they were foremost. The Sunday school in particular benefited by their care. Their family, in turn, became teachers. The sons, John and Alexander, have, as I hear from time to time, done well, while the daughters, Annie, Maggie, Kate, Minnie, and Nellie are beyond my present ken. The last was nearest my own age, and was a tall, strappin', clever lassie. The school holds many memories. Henry Boyd was schoolmaster, and Isa Wilson his assistant. Both have crossed the "divide," and I read of their "going" with regret. About ten years ago my daughter and I called, and through the kindness of the master, Mr Clark, were privileged to stand in the old building. It was full of girls and boys, but none did I know, and none knew me. As I stood they vanished, and others filled the seats. There were Isa Shand, Elsie Scott, Teenie Gaul, Elsie Urquhart, Lizzie Donaldson, Isa Donald, Mary Morison, Annie Skene, Elsie Murray, and a bevy of other rosy-cheeked lassies, smiling at me through the mists of years. Of the "sterner" sex I beheld Jock Davidson. Jamie Ledingham (Plaidy), Sandy Angus, Willie Morison, Willie Shand, Jamie Gibbon, Jamie Hay, Frank Urquhart, Geordie and Charlie Cruickshank, Jamie Carnegie, and many others. How many of them I wonder will read these lines?

About '79 or '80 there was a "roup" at Slackadale, and a great day it was. We did not get holiday, but at playtimes sped to the unwonted scene, and thoroughly enjoyed ourselves. There was a grieve there about that time known far and near as "Carnegie." Latterly he moved to Turriff, where he established a successful business as a butcher. His son James, I believe, carries it on now. Jamie was a fine laddie, and generally kept a well-sharpened knife, usually requisitioned for pencil pointing. Alex. was a brother. I remember meeting him in Turriff about twenty years ago. As I turn away from the school I cannot deny a longing glance towards the schoolhouse garden, and the little tool house where Mr Boyd used to spend many of his spare hours doing bits of joinery work. Close to the Turriff road is the smiddy, and in fancy I hear the ring of the anvil, and see Rob Hay, "Brookie," bending o'er a piece of glowing iron, or driving shoes on to some farmer's horse. Mr Hay was a scholar, and it was nothing uncommon to hear him quoting Shakespeare and other classical writers.

A thriving school 1886–1900

New people, new standards

James Elphinstone M.A. was the school's first graduate schoolmaster, and he and his wife were both certificated teachers. She helped in school, although no salary was paid to her.

Budget for Fintry School	£	s	d
Mr Elphinstone's salary	102	14	0
Miss Paterson's salary	30	0	0
Pupil Teacher	18	12	0
Books, apparatus and stationery	2	7	2½
Fuel, light and cleaning	5	7	4
Replacement /repairs to furniture and building	1	2	5
Rent, rates, taxes and insurance	1	14	6½
TOTAL	**161**	**17**	**6**

James Gaul completed his term as a pupil teacher in 1888, and achieved a good pass in the training college exam. His successor was Isabella Jane Forbes, daughter of the farmer at Milton of Craigston. In 1893, her place was taken by Nellie Chapman, again a farmer's daughter, from Slackadale. She completed the shortened indenture of two years' *'faithful and efficient service'* in December 1895, and Janet McBain, Plaidy Mill, *'who had highest marks in examination and was in all respects a suitable candidate'* became the last pupil-teacher at Fintry.

Not everyone performed as well as the pupil teachers. For example, the Sievewright family from Burnside of Delgaty were irregular attendees, with the board threatening prosecution if the children were not sent to school. When Jonathan Milne of Brackens left Fintry in August 1887 without passing Standard V, the clerk to the board contacted his father and employer and the boy returned to school.

Developments in Education

County Committees on Secondary Education were set up in 1892. Specific subjects in the schools and evening continuation classes took pupils and leavers beyond elementary levels, merit and leaving certificates were introduced, and county bursaries enabled some pupils to go on to secondary school.

Fees were abolished from October 1889, and an extra government grant was established so that ratepayers were not liable for the whole cost of education. Average attendance was now what mattered for the level of grant, the end of 'payment by results'.

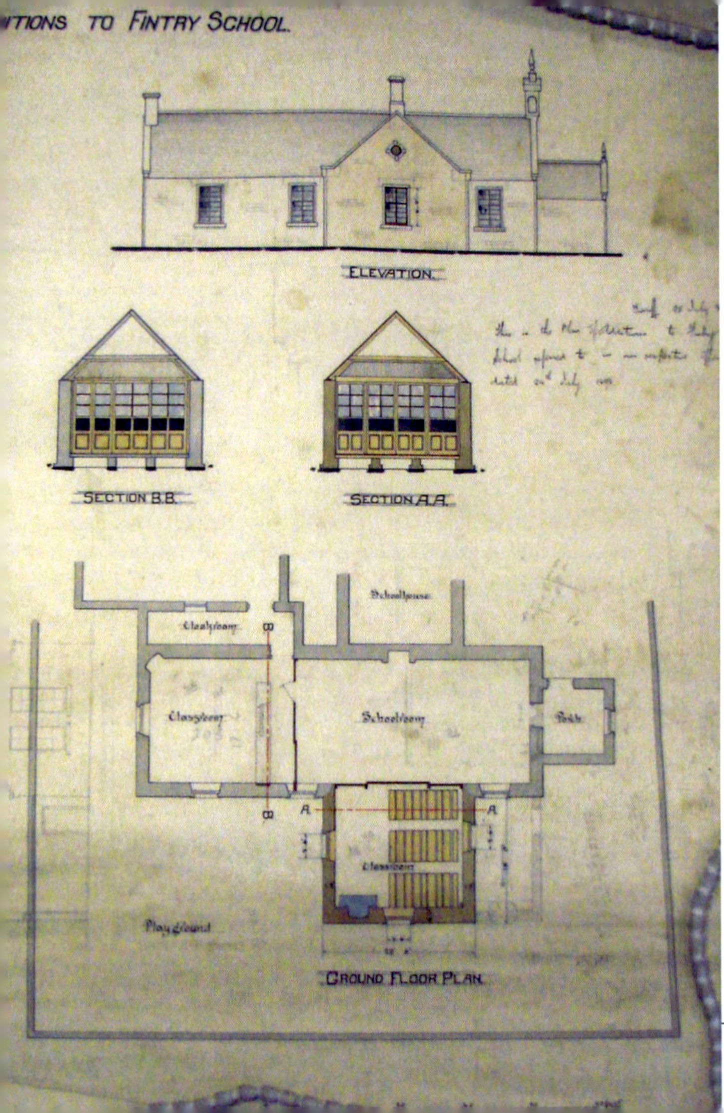

◀ **1893** third classroom

The 'Three Rs' and more

With numbers up to 140 in December 1895, an extra classroom was added to the south side of the building, and Miss Chapman, *'a most competent teacher'*, was offered a post as second assistant when her indenture ended. Her duties included teaching Music and instructing the pupil teacher under Elphinstone's supervision. In November 1898, Miss Paterson's resignation was accepted 'with great regret… after a service of nearly 15 years', on account of her ill-health. (She died, aged 36, of diabetes in 1901) *'Her work has all along been conducted with remarkable care and fidelity.'* Miss Helen Jane Smith, a certificated teacher, took charge of the infants.

In 1886–87 the board teachers condemned the exclusive use of the Royal series of readers as they had *'a crushing effect on the intellectual vision of both teachers and scholars, they were too difficult for younger pupils and dry and uninteresting for the older standards.'* They were replaced by Collins readers as, *'though somewhat more gaudy in colour than school books generally are,* [they]*… are exceedingly cheap, contain interesting material and every possible aid to intelligently comprehending the* *lessons – and are prime favourites with HM Inspectors.'*

The prize-winners in a writing competition held in December 1889 were:

Standard	First Prize	Second Prize
7	Nellie Chapman	Chrissie Clark
6	William Cranna	Fanny Elder
5	Minnie Wilson	James Ellis
4	James Ironside	Annie Leggat
3	William Tough	William Henderson
2	Margaret Craik	Jessie Murray

Elementary Science lessons included experiments with oxygen carried out by Miss Chapman assisted by the master, and the top standard was learning square roots, compound interest and some algebra in 1896. The pupil teacher had some tuition in Greek.

In physical education, the children did exercises to music with dumb bells and Indian clubs, and some senior girls attended a Dairying class at John Ledingham's Institution at Fintry. There was a great deal of repetition and blackboard drill and exams were held regularly on Fridays. *(See* APPENDIX *4: HMI Report, 1896)*

Religious instruction

When the school board made its 1898 inspection of Religious Instruction, they reported *'evidence of faithful, skilful, sympathetic teaching. A special word of commendation is due to the pleasing way in which the hymns for repetition were sung in parts: and the committee found with much satisfaction that the teachers concern themselves with the manners and behaviour of the children in the playground as well as in school.'*

However the schoolmasters wondered if *'the time had come to relieve them of the necessity of spending a large part of every morning in giving religious instruction, all more so as they are unanimously of the opinion that the method of examination has very little of religious element and simply tests to what extent the children have been drilled in historical facts.'*

A simplified syllabus was adopted by the board, but when there was a staff shortage, religious instruction was the first subject to be dropped from the timetable, followed by Poetry.

Elphinstone's successes

The first Fintry pupils to gain the new merit certificates in

1893 were J. Morrison, J. W. Morrison, and J. Ironside. The school had considerable success in the 1895 County Bursary Competition. Out of nine Fintry pupils who sat the exams, Mary Morrison, aged 14, won the £20 first bursary in Turriff district, and Helen G. Milne (16) won £4. In 1897, Agnes McBain, Alice Morrison and Bessie Hutcheon each won £4 bursaries. These enabled them to attend Turriff School for secondary education.

In April 1892, 116 ratepayers and parents at Fintry petitioned the School Board:

> *Learning that Mr Elphinstone is applying for another school and being desirous of retaining him at Fintry on account of the very high class work he is doing and the attachment of the children to him,* [we] *earnestly desire the School Board to increase his salary and so induce him to remain.*

Elphinstone stayed for another eight years, and left in April 1900 to become headmaster at King Edward School.

James Lawrence quotes a fellow-pupil, Charles Cruickshank:

> *Fintry School saw four changes of teachers during my eight years' schooling. Mr Boyd you mention, with Isa Wilson and Miss Adam. Mr Shand followed, with James Gaul as pupil teacher. Mr Brown came third, and lastly in my time Mr Elphinstone, recently retired from King-Edward school. He was teacher of all teachers, a teacher without a strap, an unknown event at Fintry school, a teacher that used brains instead of tawse, who gave a right telling off when necessary that was worse than any strap. He was a man I could never forget.*
>
> (BANFFSHIRE JOURNAL, 24 October 1922)

Some former pupils

James Gaul, farmer's son and pupil teacher, attended Aberdeen University, but left for health reasons. He worked in the sugar industry in Trinidad, Peru and Jamaica, and died in Billingham, USA, in 1944.

(*BANFFSHIRE JOURNAL,* 15 August 1944)

The pupils had a half-holiday on 8 April 1898 in honour of George Hutcheon, who graduated with first class honours in Maths and Natural Philosophy, gaining the Simpson Mathematical Prize, the Greig Natural Philosophy Prize and the Rennet Gold Medal. He became Mathematical and

Science master at Vale of Leven Academy, Alexandria, Dunbartonshire and then assistant master at the burgh grammar school in Campbeltown, Argyllshire.

(*Col. Wm. Johnston,* Roll of the Graduates of the University of Aberdeen 1860-1900)

Helen G. Milne, whose father was a shoemaker at Craigston, spent three years at the Pestalozzi Froebel Training School, Berlin. She taught in Petrograd and several other placements abroad, and returned to be teacher of languages at Kemnay Higher Grade school before becoming head of the Government Girls' School in Maritzburg, South Africa.

(*Banffshire Journal,* 5 February 1924)

In the community

The county council appointed an itinerant lecturer to take a class on agriculture in the school in the winter of 1891. Between 40 and 50 attended the first evening of this ten-lecture course, but the class was moved to Turriff the next winter.

Evening continuation classes were held in 1894 and 1895, with HMI reporting:

> *The teacher* [Elphinstone] *has drawn and kept together a very large class for this rural district. This is at once the best proof of the need of such a class, of a well selected course of lessons, and of thoroughly sound and intelligent instruction.*
>
> [The] *great majority of the pupils have returned for a second session and have thus shown their appreciation of the careful and thorough methods applied to all the subjects in the timetable.*

There was occasional use of the school for a ratepayers' meeting before a school board election, and the Fintry Ploughmen's MIA used the school regularly, to debate the issues of the day or enjoy a concert. The *Banffshire Journal* reported in April 1880 that more than 70 attended the last MIA meeting of the winter, when John Paterson of Lower Cotburn read an essay on *'Life and Economy'*. John Ledingham chaired that meeting, but sometimes a farm servant did this duty. Two other farm servants who gave talks to the MIA were Mr A. Henderson who spoke on *'Our Forefathers and their Struggles for Freedom'* in February 1882, and Mr Carnegie, in January 1883, on *'The Relation that exists between Farmers and their Servants'*. This provoked an animated discussion.

The association held the occasional dance in the school, and the Rev. AM MacLean was granted permission to use the premises on Sunday afternoons from 1891 for a religious service.

Celebrations and commemorations

There were days off for the children to attend a children's concert in January 1891 and a children's operetta in April 1896. A royal wedding earned them a day's holiday in July 1893, the Queen's Golden Jubilee (1887) afforded two days, and her Diamond Jubilee (1897) a whole week.

There were sad occasions too. The school closed for the funeral of an unnamed pupil in May 1889, and for John Ledingham's on 7 February 1900. The log book says:

> *For 24 years Mr Ledingham was a member of the School Board, and since 1857 he had been closely associated with the work carried on here. In Mr Ledingham the children of this school have lost a warm friend who was ever ready to extend many privileges to them.*

On 21 August 1891, the school celebrated its sixtieth anniversary with a picnic at Hatton Castle:

> *FINTRY PUBLIC SCHOOL –The children attending Fintry School held a grand picnic on Friday to celebrate the sixtieth anniversary of the school. Maj. Duff of Hatton very kindly placed his grounds at their disposal. The children, accompanied by parents and friends, were conveyed to Hatton in carts beautifully decorated for the occasion. These decorations were the subject of much remark on the way. On arriving, Maj. Duff, assisted by Mr Marr, gardener, proceeded to inspect the carts, sixteen in number, and to award prizes for the decorations as follows: 1 George Macrae, Whiterashes; 2 Andrew Sievewright, Hill of Muiryfold: 3 Wm. Macdonald, Ferniestripe. Mr Gammie then photographed the carts and took a group of the children.*
>
> *Mr Stewart having provided refreshments, the usual games were set agoing, and engaged in with great spirits. Several enthusiastic friends scattered sweets broadcast, and coppers were lavishly distributed. Aunt Sally and her sister got great attention, and swings, &c. were largely patronised. A feature of the day and the procession was the music supplied by three pipers. After a march through the beautiful gardens, tea was served and sweets distributed. Each child also received a suitable gift. Having been drawn up in front of the Castle, the children sang the 'Auld Hoose' and*

gave hearty cheers for Major and Mrs Duff and Master Duff. Major Duff, in reply, alluded to the interesting occasion, and trusted that the school might long continue to be a centre of usefulness, and proposed a vote of thanks to the teachers, which was cordially given. Singing was then engaged in, and the usual vote of thanks to all who had contributed to the day's enjoyment. Major Hutcheon represented the School Board. Before leaving, Major Duff gave each child a bag of sweets. The journey through Turriff assumed the form of a triumphal procession, and seemed to give pleasure to all the onlookers. Carts were sent from Mill of Fintry, Slap, Upper and Lower Cotburn, Badentyre, Hillhead of Muiryfold, Brackens, Whiterashes, Back Plaidy, Ferniestripe, Slackadale and Midtown.

(BANFFSHIRE JOURNAL, 28 August 1891)

From welfare to war 1900 –1919

With Turriff a 'Central School' drawing in some children for secondary education, the three country schools, Fintry, Ardmiddle and Birkenhills were put on equal footing. Fintry had enjoyed larger numbers and better status than the others, but its staff numbers were now reduced from three to two.

Supplementary courses, to be taken after children had passed the Merit Certificate, replaced the specific subjects when the leaving age was raised to 14 in 1901. Drawing and Nature Knowledge became compulsory subjects.

Exemption by passing an exam had been abolished and the board now decided each case on its merits.

When Miss Macfarlane (Fintry) and Mr Roy (Ardmiddle) sought an increase in salary in 1902, Mr George Hutcheon's committee on staff and salaries declared:

> *We thoroughly appreciate the services of [these assistant teachers] but feel the schools of Fintry and Ardmiddle are costing sufficient already and that energetic teachers in our side schools should merely look upon them as stepping stones to more important appointments…*

A new schoolhouse

Improvements were made to lighting in 1905 and hand-washing facilities were installed in a new porch, but the main building project was a fine new schoolhouse, paid for with a loan from central government. The surviving portion of the old schoolhouse became a store.

For the senior pupils

In 1900 Fintry was the only country school in the area to send pupils to Turriff to sit the Leaving Certificate, when the school had one pass in Arithmetic and one fail in English. Soon the SED was concerned about the number of Fintry pupils leaving without gaining even the lower Merit Certificate.

James Clark, schoolmaster, complained that the approved course for Fintry had no languages or maths, which limited the children's choices of future occupation.

By 1905 he was permitted to teach Latin and French to selected pupils who could not attend Turriff School, if their

▶ **1907** new porch added

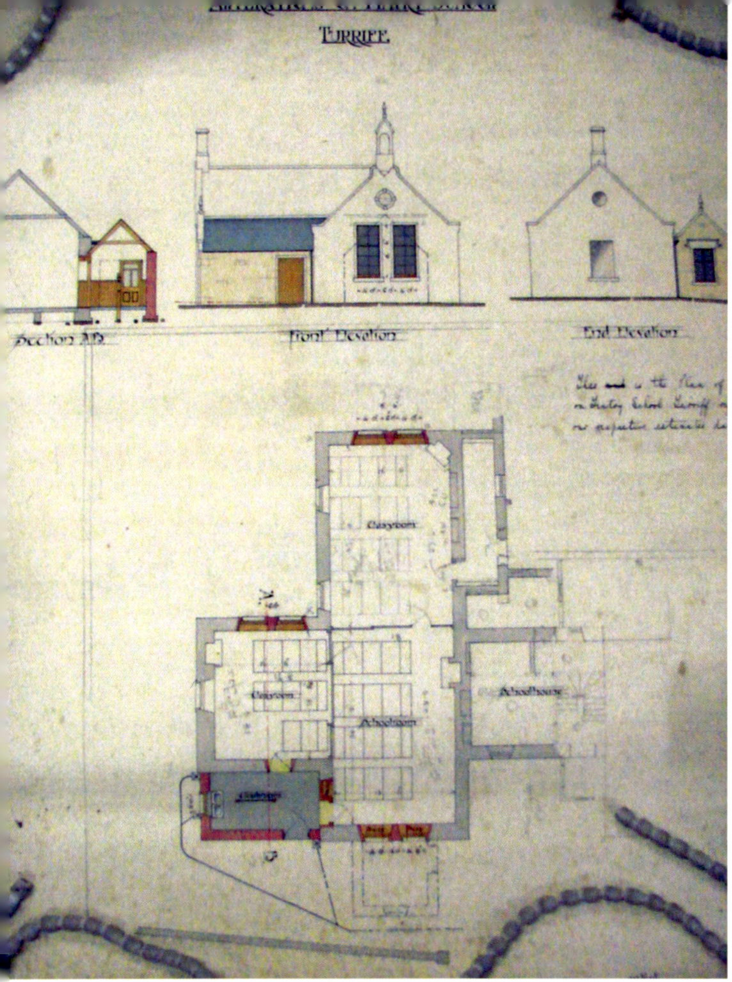

parents wished. The Fintry MIA made part of its library (around 300 books kept in the school) available for the supplementary course, but complaints about damage to them led to their being withdrawn. Clark then obtained a grant of books from Coats School Libraries, Paisley, and the board recommended its other schools do the same.

An attempt to keep the senior pupils interested was initiated in 1911, once the technical building at Turriff was completed. HM Inspector Philip suggested that over-12s could walk to Turriff from the country schools to have Technical instruction, a distance of three to six miles each way - out of the eligible 12 boys and 11 girls in Fintry there were no takers.

Later in the year, J Duncan of the Crown Hotel was hired to convey pupils weekly to Turriff for Woodwork and Cookery, and this continued for part of every year until the war.

The master taught Shorthand and Typing continuation evening classes, and an Agricultural class was held over the winter of 1909, ending with an *'At Home'* in the school.

Missing school

A five-year-old girl, Chrissie Jane Gaul of Whiterashes, unable through poor health to walk the distance to school, was exempted from attendance over the winter months. Maggie Keilloh, Slackadale, aged 13, was allowed two days off per week to look after her mother who was *'in delicate health'*. Maria Walker, Lower Cotburn, was refused two weeks off to go to harvest, but Lily Sievewright, Badentyre, was granted exemption because of her mother's poverty on condition the mother could get a *'place'* for her.

George Penny, Crossfields, and David Keilloh were granted exemptions to work. John Innes, Kinbate was granted exemption to help his grandfather on his farm. In 1913, Maggie Barclay, Upper Cotburn, got exemption for harvest only if J. K. Ledingham promised to see she returned afterwards.

Teachers in trouble

Alexander Keilloh, farm grieve at Slackadale, complained, in December 1902, that Clark had struck his son, also Alexander, on the hand with a slate, to his slight injury. The boy had then refused to take punishment because of his injury, and had been allegedly kicked and expelled. While Clark admitted striking the boy with the slate, he said he had expelled him for his refusal to take punishment, and would not take him back until he admitted telling a lie to his parents. The board felt bound to support Clark on the question of discipline but felt he had erred in striking the boy with a slate. They ruled that when the boy returned to school he should submit to punishment but not be asked to apologise.

In February 1915 James Pennie of Burnside of Delgaty alleged that he had been *'ill-used'* by Clark, who replied that he had had to punish the boy for insolent behaviour towards Miss Chapman. He also objected to Pennie's exemption. The board agreed that the exemption be refused, that Pennie might be sent to Turriff School and that his request for exemption would be reconsidered if he did well.

On the other hand, Clark had to advise Miss Macfarlane in April 1902, soon after she started teaching at Fintry, to use a strap instead of striking the heads of the children.

Health and welfare

There was growing national realisation that the physical well-being of children was in need of improvement, and increased emphasis on Drill was the immediate consequence in the schools. Doctors were entitled to close schools to prevent the spread of diphtheria, measles and influenza.

After cases of diphtheria in 1903, when Fintry was described as *'dirty'*, the classrooms were redecorated with paint rather than distemper, which was thought to attract dust, and cleaning rules were introduced. One child was described as *'in no fit condition to sit beside other children'* by the doctor and reported to the sanitary inspector.

Lessons on Hygiene and Temperance were introduced. After an outbreak of a *'worm pest'* in the desks in December 1905, the sanitary inspector instructed that food should not be kept in the desks, and JK Ledingham and the board officer oversaw eradication.

The Education Act of 1908 made medical inspection compulsory and the Fintry children had their first inspection on 7 June 1910, with the school visitors present.

Some highlights

Bursaries for academic secondary education were won by Lily Chessar (1901) and Jessie Cowie (1907). Prize-giving was a feature of the year, with prizes given for regular attendance, and presented by the board chairman, a school visitor or Mrs Pollard Urquhart of Craigston Castle.

The school was struck by lightning in 1903. Little damage was done, but the children were shaken and the event became part of the oral history of the school, re-told even in the 1950s.

A picnic was to be held in Turriff for King Edward's coronation in 1902, with a thousand children attending, but the day was *'drenching rain'* so the country children were taken to the Parish Hall for sports, and the town children had their event on the following Saturday. The school procured carts and visited Bostock and Wombwell's Menagerie in Turriff in 1912.

A chat with a centenarian

Maggie Ann Chapman was born on 1 May 1909 and attended Fintry School from 1915. She started school aged six, walking from Burnside of Delgaty with her older sister, Bella. They walked to school by Brackens and Kinminty, a *'fair walk'*. Maggie recalled fellow pupils Margaret Thain, Jimmy Barclay, Joan Barclay, Jimmy Cheyne, Margaret Cheyne and Willie Massie.

She remembered playing, *'aye outside'*, and sometimes barefoot. She smiled on recollecting playing *'hopping' beds'* and thinks she may have skipped and played hide and seek. *'We used to play among the stooks, an' crawl in atween them'* and got in trouble for knocking them all down.

She was not often off school *'nae weel'*, the family were quite healthy. She remembered scraping a turnip, to eat going home from school.

Of her teachers, Miss Chapman and Miss Fowlie: '*I got on with them all. We would have got into trouble if we didna. There was a fair class, bigger than there is now: there's no sae mony going'*. She thought the children at school behaved *'real weel'; you got the strap if you didn't behave'*, but Maggie did not remember getting the strap herself. She liked school. She carried her *'dinner'* to school – a slice of *'loaf'* and butter, *'nane o' yer jam'*.

The First World War

School attendance decreased from autumn 1915 onwards, especially at busy times on the farms. Some boys were exempted for harvest only, but many had their education ended for good. They included Alexander Walker (on 12 March 1915), William Innes, Kinbate (2 May 1915, a *'good scholar'* who had *'passed the qualifying exam')*, William Will, Hill of Cotburn (14 January 1916), William Largue, Brackens (6 March 1916, aged 13½), John Cranna, Fintry Smithy (2 October 1916 for harvest only, at Fintry Farm), James Barclay, Whiterashes (8 January 1917, aged 13 years), George Duncan, Ferniestripe (20 March 1917, aged 13) and James Scorgie, Cotburn and William Taylor, Plaidy Station (both 4 March 1918). The youngest boys were exempted on condition they attended two years' continuation classes.

Girls were exempted too - for example: Margaret Barclay (11 September 1914), and Maggie Imlah and Agnes Hay (16 June 1916); no reason is given, but *THE WAR BOOK OF TURRIFF* notes that some girls were employed to do *'men's work'*.

Classes in Turriff were discontinued after August 1917 as shortage of labour meant there was no driver available to take the children to Turriff for the classes. Clark asked for a sewing machine after the technical instruction was stopped, noting that Ardmiddle and Birkenhills had one each, but there is no record of his receiving one.

After 1915, certificates were substituted for prizes. A series of food economy classes was held on four alternate days in June-July 1917 at Greeness and Fintry. About 20 adults and a *'good number'* of children attended at Fintry. The county's medical inspection scheme was no longer free after April 1915, and was suspended within the year, but the Turriff board continued eye tests, and engaged the district nurse to examine children with any sort of health problem.

Serving their country

At the end of October 1918, influenza broke out in the Fintry area and the school was closed from 5 to 19 November, so after over four years when the war is never mentioned in the log book, there is no mention of the Armistice either. Yet Mr Clark must have been amongst many who felt immense relief, as he had three sons, former pupils at Fintry, serving in the forces.

Robert James Clark, MB ChB, RAMC, served as a captain in England and France and was gassed and invalided home from the trenches at Bullecourt; Alexander Milne Clark, bank clerk, served with the Royal Naval Division on HMS Minotaur and HMS Shannon as a leading signalman and assistant schoolmaster in the North Sea, the Atlantic and the Arctic Oceans, and took part in the Battle of Jutland five days after first going aboard a warship. Their young brother, Allan Burness Clark, medical student, served with the RNVR for six months from September 1918 as a surgeon sub-lieutenant in the North Sea where he witnessed the surrender of the German fleet.

Other Fintry former pupils who served were the brothers James and John Gaul, Whiterashes, and John Ledingham, Fintry. He was commissioned from the ranks in 1917. Five of six Leggat brothers from Gairnieston served, with one being killed and another winning the Military Medal. Albert Hutcheon, Cotburn, won the Military Cross for conspicuous gallantry at Vimy in April 1917 and was

totally blinded by shrapnel three weeks later.
(Information from THE WAR BOOK OF TURRIFF *and* TWELVE MILES ROUND*)*

The end of the school boards

The Education (Scotland) Act of 1918 abolished the board system. In its 46 years the Turriff board managed the schools in Turriff and at Fintry, Ardmiddle and Birkenhills, overseeing much new building in spite of financial strictures in running costs.

Several members of the Fintry community had served on the board, namely John Ledingham from 1873 to 1897, his son John Knox Ledingham from 1903 to 1914, John Hutcheon, Lower Cotburn, from 1882 to 1894 and his son Harry from 1914 until the end of the Board. William Davidson of Burnside House also served from 1911.

The 1920s

In the classroom

A lack of reading books left John Carrell setting Standard VI to reading Lessons in Hygiene soon after he came to Fintry, but books arrived in January 1921 with new maps of Scotland and England, Europe and Asia.

In October 1925, cookery was *'still being carried out under difficulty, there being no tables'*, but from the following September the advanced division had both Cookery and Science lessons.

When the authority set up an economies committee in 1922, one of its first actions was to cut out funding for prizes and school libraries. After much pleading from teachers, prizes were reinstated in 1926, for merit and attendance.

Mrs WK Leggat of Yonderton presented the prizes in 1927, then Mrs Mary Logan (wife of the United Free Church minister in Turriff and a member of the education authority and Turriff SMC from 1922) the next two years.

The Education (Scotland) Act 1918 set up an Education Authority for each county council. Overall control was centred in the Scottish Education Department (SED) in Edinburgh, and the largest share of funding came from the central Education (Scotland) Fund.

Aberdeenshire's first elected representatives from the Turriff area were the Rev. Alexander Duncan (The Manse, Auchterless) and Rev. Alexander Macalpine (UFC Manse, Cuminestown), Robert Paterson (retired farmer, of 'Turra Coo' fame, and former member of Turriff school board) and John Neish Ritchie, Schoolhill, Turriff (merchant and former school board member). Local school management committees (SMCs) were set up with parent, teacher, and religious representation.

A survey of educational provision in the county concluded: 'When the age limit is raised, Steinmanhill, St Katherine's, Garmond, Fisherie and Fintry would be primary schools purely'. The leaving age rise to 15 was in fact delayed until after the Second World War, and Fintry continued to provide post-primary education until 1937, through supplementary courses and then the advanced division.

In 1930 a report on post-primary education favoured keeping children as near home as possible, 'if the evils due to migration of farm servants are to be reduced to a minimum'. Fintry was then designated a primary school, but for those children not 'promoted' to Turriff secondary school, its advanced division provided a one-year Domestic Science course, with the boys taken to Turriff twice a week for Woodwork and Science.

She donated silver dux medals in 1929, when the senior winner was John Morrison, Brackens and the junior one Kenneth Morrison, Cotburn.

Kenneth Milne, county librarian, visited Fintry in March 1928 to set up a branch, and from then on, books were exchanged three times a year when the library van called. General readers were also issued to the schools and used as additional class readers or for silent reading. Miss Buchan noted in October 1928 that the *'continuous readers from the education authority are much appreciated'*.

Miss Buchan took the senior pupils to see *Ben Hur* at the cinema in Turriff in April 1928. This counted as an educational visit, as did participation in the Turriff music festival in May 1928, when Fintry pupils gained three first-class and three second-class certificates in elocution. The pupils attended the education authority's concert in 1927, the first of a series initiated *'with the view primarily of fostering in school children a love of things musical'*. A violinist, an elocutionist and two vocalists *'gave a splendid performance in the Picture House'* in the afternoon for the children from all the local schools. Mozart and Handel's music, Kipling's Just So stories and AA Milne's poems featured, with other items.

Inspections

The HMI report of April 1927 notes:

> *In the Junior Room the work is energetically carried on, and the methods employed are modern, stimulating and effective. In the Senior Room distinct progress is being made. Nature Study and Observation are quite unusually good and deserve special commendation. English Composition shows some considerable improvement and may be expected to show further advance from an increased supply of reading material. The walls should be fully utilised for the display of geographical and historical maps, charts and pictures.*

Two years later, there were some improvements, some lack of success:

> *In both sections of the school, the work is carried on with energy, faithfulness and success, and the display of diagrams, pictures, charts and collections of flowers merits special commendation. In the upper classes more time should be given to the study of the elements of formal grammar, and the teaching of singing by note seems to depend too much on the use of the piano.*

Miss Gaul and infants 1929: On the right in the background can be seen the original school, used as a store, and on the left the 1907 schoolhouse. 1929 – Teacher Miss Agnes Gaul. **Back:** Kenneth Morrison, George Wilson, Robert Barron, Norman Leggat, James Taylor, George Cheyne, Bertie Gray, James Cheyne, James Ironside, unknown, Norman Lorimer, unknown. **Middle:** Margaret Ledingham, Mina Cowie, Lily Leslie, Kathleen McDonald, Margaret Skinner, Peter Cheyne, unknown, Ruby Mair, unknown, Peggy Thomson, ? Cheyne. **Front:** Bessie McDonald, Molly Cheyne, Isobel Ledingham, Maydith Wood, Annie Taylor, unknown, Caroline Leggat, Margaret Wilson, unknown, Annie Leslie, 'Doddie' Taylor.

Pupils come and go

Many children were admitted from other local schools at term-time; fourteen left the district in May 1921. Some moved only a few miles and returned soon afterwards. The Murdoch family came from St Margaret's (Episcopal) School, in Aberdeen. Two brothers, Edward Cardwell Alexander and Erskine Alexander, from Tower Bank School, Portobello arrived in May 1920, but were marked *'gone to Canada'* in April 1922. Dolly Shea emigrated to Canada in November 1920.

Hygiene and temperance

Cases of *'the itch'* and ringworm continued, and *'sore eyes'* were common, as were mumps, measles and diphtheria; a whole family was sent home for a fortnight with skin disease. A qualifying class pupil, Margaret Thain, died of tuberculosis in May 1925. Scarlet fever caused three pupils to be absent for three months over the winter of 1928–9, and 50 per cent of the pupils were absent with whooping-cough in June 1929.

The Scottish Band of Hope gave talks in school under such headings as *'Alcohol and the Brain'* (Sept 1921 and 1922), *'Temperance'* (March 1925) and *'Everything in Its Place'* (Feb 1928).

Empire Day

This was inaugurated in 1923, with a message from the king and queen sent to all head teachers to read to their pupils on 25 May. In 1925 Provost Christie spoke to the pupils on *'Patriotism and Loyalty'*, the next year the Rev. Logan gave an address on *'Good Citizenship'*.

The children performed recitations and songs - *'The Union Jack'* and Kipling's *Recessional* (with the refrain, 'Lest we forget') were favourites. The national anthem was sung and the Union Jack saluted, after which the children got a half-holiday.

Social life in and around the school

The *Banffshire Journal* reported the school's 1921 Christmas party, where children's games and tea were followed by a concert programme of 'songs, recitations and step dancing', then gifts from the Christmas tree.

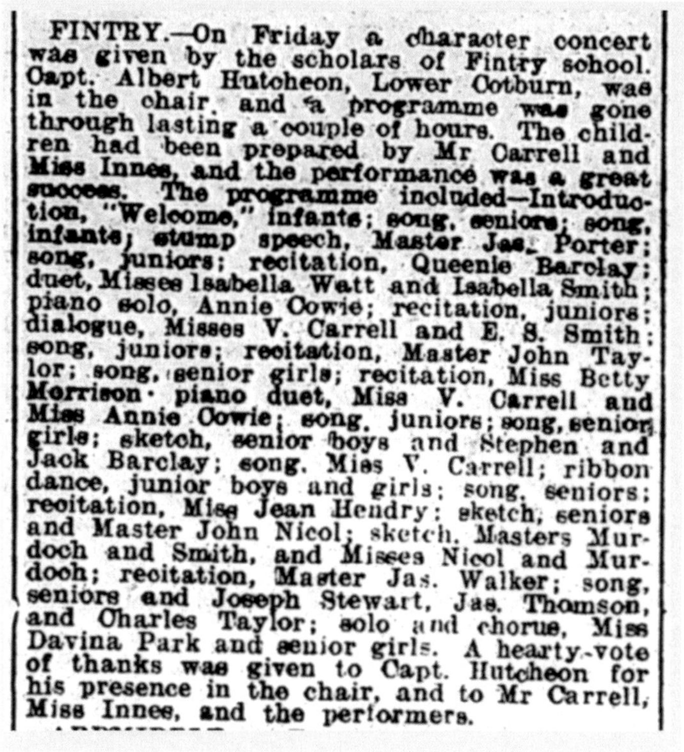

FINTRY.—On Friday a character concert was given by the scholars of Fintry school. Capt. Albert Hutcheon, Lower Cotburn, was in the chair and a programme was gone through lasting a couple of hours. The children had been prepared by Mr Carrell and Miss Innes, and the performance was a great success. The programme included—Introduction, "Welcome," infants; song, seniors; song, infants; stump speech, Master Jas. Porter; song, juniors; recitation, Queenie Barclay; duet, Misses Isabella Watt and Isabella Smith; piano solo, Annie Cowie; recitation, juniors; dialogue, Misses V. Carrell and E. S. Smith; song, juniors; recitation, Master John Taylor; song, senior girls; recitation, Miss Betty Morrison; piano duet, Miss V. Carrell and Miss Annie Cowie; song, juniors; song, senior girls; sketch, senior boys and Stephen and Jack Barclay; song, Miss V. Carrell; ribbon dance, junior boys and girls; song, seniors; recitation, Miss Jean Hendry; sketch, seniors and Master John Nicol; sketch, Masters Murdoch and Smith, and Misses Nicol and Murdoch; recitation, Master Jas. Walker; song, seniors and Joseph Stewart, Jas. Thomson, and Charles Taylor; solo and chorus, Miss Davina Park and senior girls. A hearty vote of thanks was given to Capt. Hutcheon for his presence in the chair, and to Mr Carrell, Miss Innes, and the performers.

Character Concert 1922 *Banffshire Journal*

Another concert was organised in the school with artistes from Turriff in April 1928 by Miss Buchan, Miss Gaul and the MIA Committee to raise money for the children's prize and picnic fund.

Visits to circuses, menageries and a visit to the school from a travelling ventriloquist all took place. A summer picnic was held at Craigston Castle in June 1929 when the children were marched from the school to the castle, led by Mr James Duncan, Burnside, playing the bagpipes.

John Ledingham applied to use the school for a Sunday school at the end of 1919, and in January 1920 Mrs Ledingham organised a concert and dance there in aid of the Fund for Demobilised Soldiers' Recreation Hall in Turriff.

The Fintry branch of the MIA had over 100 members by the end of the decade; Miss Robertson, infant teacher, talked to the group on *'How the Home can Help the School'* in January 1921, a fancy dress ball attended by over 100 people was held in February 1928 in aid of the Aberdeen Hospitals Scheme, and a ladies' sketch night featured Miss Buchan and Miss Gaul in March 1928. The MIA helped with donations towards school parties and picnics.

When the Fintry branch of the Scottish Women's Rural

A FINTRY ENTERTAINMENT.—While it was probably the last entertainment to be held this season in the district the concert which took place at Fintry school on Friday will be looked upon as one of the most successful. Organised by Miss Buchan, headmistress, and Miss Gaul, assistant, and the committee of the M.I.A., it attracted, notwithstanding the fact that the evening was inclement, a large audience of parents and others who have the school children's interests at heart. They appreciated the fact that by their coming forward they were giving their support to a worthy cause, the prize and picnic fund. Mr W. K. Leggat, Yonderton, local representative on the School Committee, made a genial chairman. At the start of the proceedings he expressed his gratification at the splendid attendance and said it was right they should do something for the benefit of the children in that way. The programme was sustained by a party from Turriff. Miss Normah Smith, soprano, gave pleasing renderings of "Daffodils" and "Billy Bo," and she was also charmingly heard in a duet "The Keys of Heaven," with Mr W. Ironside. Miss I. G. Mitchell, contralto, sang with fine effect "Turn ye to me" and "The Peat Fire Flame." The comic element was sustained by Mr Ironside, who appeared in various characterisations, while Mr Sweenie Robertson, with his conjuring tricks, proved amusing and entertaining. Special mention

MIA concert for school funds, 1928 *Banffshire Journal*

▶ Banffshire Journal, 7 March, 1922

Institute (WRI) was inaugurated in 1928 it also used the school for its meetings and drama festivals. The community got together in 1929 to hold a midsummer dance to raise funds for the children's Christmas treat: 'There was a record attendance and the drawings were gratifying'.

The wedding of Princess Mary in February 1922 was perhaps the biggest celebration of the decade. Turriff town and parish councils combined to organise a lavish entertainment for around 750 local children:

> *CHILDREN'S ENTERTAINMENT.- Tuesday, the day of the Royal marriage, came with bright sunshine and dry atmosphere […] From Fintry the children, under charge of Mr Carell [sic], were conveyed by Mr Morrison, Mr Leggat, Gairnieston; Mr Leggat, Yonderton; Mr Leggat [sic], Fintry; Mr Cowie, Backhill; Mr Smith, Whiterashes; Mr Cowie, Kinminty, and Mr Morrice, Craigston […] The Town Hall was crowded to its utmost capacity with all these children (from all the area's schools). As they entered, each child received a bag and a cup to hold the tea. […] Rev. D MacLaren was called upon to open the meeting. He gave out the 2nd Paraphrase, and the verses were shown on the screen and these were sung by the children, after which Mr MacLaren led in prayer.* (extract, BANFFSHIRE JOURNAL, 7 March, 1922)

CHILDREN'S ENTERTAINMENT.—Tuesday, the day of the Royal marriage, came with bright sunshine and dry atmosphere, an example of Queen's weather. There was much stir in the town and flags flew from staffs and windows, making a gay show in the bright breeze. The children were assembled and brought into town in good time for the afternoon's entertainment. The children from Ardmiddle school, under charge of Mr Mackie, Mrs Mackie and Miss Finlayson, were conveyed in a number of cars kindly lent for the occasion by Mr Wilson Henry, Turriff; Mr Marr, Turriff; Mr Cruickshank, Mill of Laithers; Mr Slessor, Raecloch; Mr Campbell, Ardmiddle; Mr Cruickshank, Hillside, and Mr Cassie, Bankhills. The pupils from Birkenhills school, in charge of Mr Macleod, Miss Murcar and Miss Singer, were conveyed by motor waggons kindly lent by Mr R. Paterson of Lendrum. From Fintry the children, under charge of Mr Carell, were conveyed by Mr Morrison, Mr Leggat, Gairnieston; Mr Leggat, Yonderton; Mr Leggat, Fintry; Mr Cowie, Backhill; Mr Smith, Whiterashes; Mr Cowie, Kinminty, and Mr Morrice, Craigston. Miss Milne brought the children from Dunlugas in vehicles, lent by Mr Towler, Mr Strachan, Mr Grieve and Mr Aivars, in charge of the Dunlugas van. The children of the infant department of the secondary school were present under Mr Melvin, Mrs Buchanan and Miss Ledingham. The Town Hall was crowded to its utmost capacity with all these children. As they entered each child received a bag and a cup to hold the tea. These were in charge of Mr Johnston, burgh officer, and Mr Jerram, janitor of the burgh school. The Town Council were represented by Provost Stewart, who presided over the meeting, Bailie Watson, Mr Christie, Mrs Logan, and Mr D. Davidson, and the Parish Council was represented by Mr Kindness, Mr Henry Howie, Haughs, and Mr Hay, Mains of Laithers. Rev. D. MacLaren was called on to open the meeting. He gave out the 2nd Paraphrase, and the verses were shown on the screen and these were sung by the children, after which Mr MacLaren led in prayer. Provost Stewart in a short speech reminded the children of the day and occasion and hoped they would enjoy the entertainment and long remember the occasion, ending by wishing long life and happiness to the Princess Mary and her husband. Tea was then served by the girls in the three highest classes of the secondary school, and full justice was done to the contents of the bags. Following this was a cinema display beginning with an amusing piece "Brass Buttons," and followed by a farcical sketch. As most of the country children were seeing a cinema for the first time, they showed their appreciation by hearty laughter. At the conclusion, Provost Stewart proposed a vote of thanks to Mrs Logan and the members of the committee who had arranged the entertainment, to Mr George Hutcheon of Gask, who had generously given the oranges, and Mr Booth of Kinermit, who had kindly given the milk. Mr Melvin moved a vote of thanks to Provost Stewart for his activities that day, and for having presented the bags of cakes they had all partaken of. The children sang "God Save the King" and as they passed out each child received an orange. The music during the entertainment was by Miss Barrie. In the evening the older pupils of the burgh were entertained in the same way, and an audience of four hundred was present. Mr Melvin, headmaster, moved a vote of thanks to all those who had provided the entertainment and to the committee who had made the arrangements and carried them through. On Wednesday the same film was repeated, and the hall was open to the public. An audience of three hundred and fifty or more was present and a silver collection was taken to help to defray any extra charges. Provost Stewart in opening the performance expressed his appreciation of the kindness of the Cinema Company in granting the use of the hall free for the performances. The Royal marriage has thus been fittingly commemorated, and all the youth of Turriff and parish will retain an exceedingly pleasant memory of the occasion.

Hard times in the 1930s

The Education (Scotland) Act of 1929 abolished the education authorities and transferred their powers to education committees in each city or county council.

Their responsibilities were basically the same as those of the former authorities - the education, medical inspection and treatment, the feeding and clothing where necessary of the school children of the area, and the continuing provision of public libraries. The school management committees continued. Major Ledingham joined the Turriff one in January 1931.

The new regime came into existence just as the Great Depression took effect. Aberdeenshire's education budget suffered annual cuts of up to 23 percent between 1931 and 1938 with strict allocation of funds to projects such as improving heating and sanitation for rural schools, and the installation of 'cookhouses'.

At Fintry water closets were finally installed along with a shelter shed for the girls in early 1937. Apart from gravelling the playground in 1931 and placing wire netting over the windows in 1934 the only other improvement was the supply in 1938 of two hot air stoves taken from the old school at New Byth, to replace the open fires.

Hot dinner scheme

Maj. W. K. Leggat chaired a meeting of parents on 15 December 1930, which agreed that a hot dinner scheme should be set up for the winter, at a charge of ½d per child per week, with no family paying more than 6d per week. A committee of four women, Mmes Leslie, Park, Morrison and Wilson, with Messrs Leggat and Ledingham, was appointed to assist the teachers in carrying out the arrangements.

While the education committee provided utensils and paid the cook, and Turriff shopkeepers supplied meat and groceries, local farmers donated the potatoes and vegetables, and Captain Pollard-Urquhart of Craigston Castle gave a weekly gift of rabbits. Mr Cowie of Brackens gave milk free of charge for the cocoa every year.

From November 1931 to March 1932 an average of 60 children out of a roll of 66 were served with soup each day. The menu at the beginning was potato soup on Mondays and Fridays, pea soup on Tuesdays, broth on Wednesdays and lentil soup on Thursdays, but a little variety crept in with cocoa instead of soup every second day and bradies or

Peter Cowie (Kinminty) with milk cart, on Brackens road 1935

ember
1934

		Nov. 23	Nov 30	Dec 7	Dec. 14	Dec 21	Jan 4	Jan 11	Jan 18	Jan 25	Feb. 1	Feb. 8	Feb 15	Feb 22	Mar 1	Mar 8	Mar 15	Mar 22
an	4	–	8	4	4	4	3	6	6	6	6	6	6	6	6	6	6	6
yne St.	4	6	6	6	6	6	3	6	6	6	2½	6	6	6	6	6	6	6
ne V.C.	2	5	4	5	5	5	2	5	5	5	5	4	5	5	5	5	5	5
kshank	1	–	4	2½	2½	2½	1	2½	2½	2½	2½	2½	2½	2½	2½	2½	2½	2½
sie	1	–	–	1	2½	2½	1	2½	2½	–	–		2½	2½	2½	2	2½	2½
vidson	1	2½	2	2½	2	2	1½	2½	2½	2½	2½	2½	2½	2½	2½	2½	2½	2½
ay	3	1/-	1/-	1/-	1/-	1/-	6	1/-	1/-	1/-	1/-	1/-	1/-	1/-	1/-	1/-	1/-	1/-
slie	2	5	4	5	5	5	2	5	5	5	5	3½	5	5	5	5	5	5
ingham	4	6	6	6	6	6	3	6	6	6	6	6	6	6	6	6	6	6
ggat	3	6	6	6	6	6	3	6	6	2½	2	2	2	6	6	6	6	6
onald	3	6	6	6	6	6	2	6	6	6	–	3	6	5	6	6	6	6
ntash	3	3	6	6	6	6	3	6	6	6	6	6	6	6	6	6	6	6
owlan	2	5	4	5	5	5	2	5	5	5	5	2½	5					
aughton	1	2½	2	2½	2½	2½	1	2½	2½	2½	2½							
lor	4	6	6	6	6	6	3	6	6	6	–	6	6	6	6	6	6	6
nner	3	6	6	6	6	6	3	6	6	6	6	6	6	6	6	6	6	6
ith	1	2½	2	2½	2	2½	1	2½	2½	2½								
clair	4	6	6	6	6	6	3	6	6	6		6	6	6	6	6	6	6
od	2	5	4	5	5	5	2	5	5	5	3	3	3	5	5	5	5	5

		Nov 23	Nov 30	Dec 7	Dec 14	Dec 21	Jan 4	Jan 11	Jan 18	Jan 25	Feb 1	Feb 8	Feb 15	Feb 22	Mar 1	Mar 8	Mar 15	Mar 22
Davie	4	6	6	6	6	6	3	6	6	6	6	6	6	6	6	6	6	6
Will	4	6	6	6	6	6	3	6	6	6	6	6	6	6	6	6	6	6
Cranna	1	2½	2	2½	2	2½	1	2½	2½	2½	2½	–	2	2½	2½	2½	2½	2½
Bruce	1	2½	2	2½	2½	2½	1	2½	2½	2½	2½	1	2½	2½	2½	2½	2½	2½
Mitchell	1	2½	2	2½	2	2½	1	2½	2½	2½	–	3	2½	2½	2½	2½	2	2½
Morri		2½	2	2½	2½	2½	1	2½	–	2½	2½	2½	2½	2½	2½	2½	2½	2½
Paterson		2½	2	2	3	2½	1	2½	2½	2½	2½	–	3	2½	2½	2½	2½	[illegible]
McBain		–	–	–	6	6	3	6	6	6	6	6	6	6	6	6	6	6
Essemont												3½	2½	2	2	2½	2½	[illegible]
		9/1	9/6	9/11	10/2½	10/6½	5/11½	10/9	10/6½	10/3	8/1	8/11	9/2½	10/-	10/1	10/1	10/1	

◀ **Fintry families** taking hot dinners 1934-35

pies on Thursdays. *'The soup was made in the wash-house boiler, and is served to the children in the cooking-room'* (the third classroom).

Hot Dinners Scheme 1934-5

INCOME	£	S	D
In Bank	13	17	5
From Sale of Hot Dinners	8	3	7½
Total	**22**	**1**	**0½**

EXPENDITURE	£	S	D
To Mr Stewart, for groceries and bradies	7	5	0
To Mr Cheyne, for butcher meat	2	15	0
Total	**10**	**4**	**0**
To Mr Howie, for carrots		4	0
Balance	**11**	**17**	**0½**
In bank	11	13	5
In hand		3	7½

The promoters tried to share their trade among the Turriff shops, as long as delivery was possible, for not all the shops had vans. Miss Buchan kept the minutes and accounts book, which contains tables of the children taking the meals and the amount paid weekly, with lists of the farmers who gave supplies, and the annual income and expenditure.

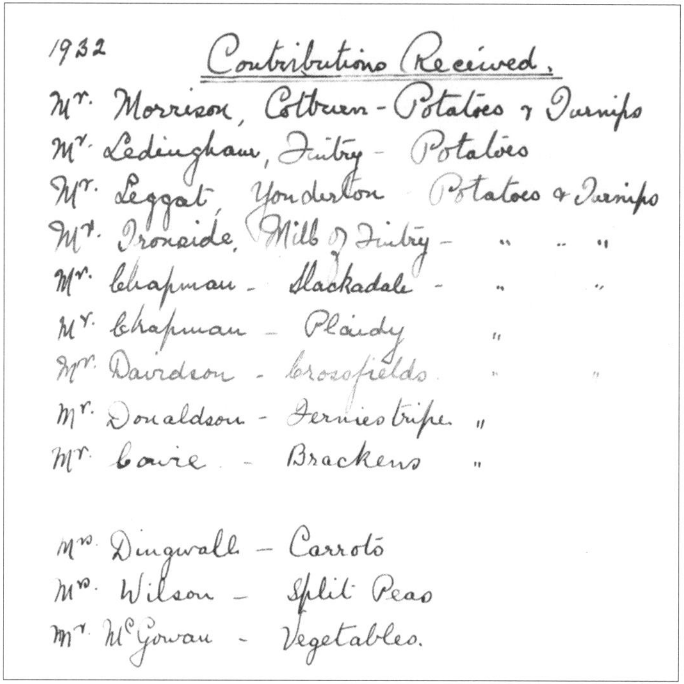

1932 Contributions Received.

Mr. Morrison, Coltbuen - Potatoes & Turnips
Mr. Ledingham, Fintry - Potatoes
Mr. Leggat, Yonderton Potatoes & Turnips
Mr. Ironside, Mill of Fintry - " " "
Mr. Chapman - Slackadale - " "
Mr. Chapman - Plaidy "
Mr. Davidson - Crossfields " "
Mr. Donaldson - Ferniestripe "
Mr. Cowie - Brackens "

Mrs. Dingwall - Carrots
Mrs. Wilson - Split Peas
Mr. McGowan - Vegetables.

Hot dinners contributions received

The minutes of March 1932 state: *'It was noted that Fintry School had the highest percentage of attendance in the area, [...] this was partly attributed to the good health maintained amongst the children by having a hot meal daily'*.

1931–2 infants. See the rough gravel surface to the playground. **Back**: George Will, James McIntosh/James Sinclair, ? Barron, unknown, George McNaughton, ? Rodger, Peter or Willie Duncan, James Cheyne, Alex Mair, George Maitland, Peter or Willie Duncan, Billy Lorimer. **Middle**: unknown, Kathleen McGowan, ? Andrew, Betty Taylor, Isobel Ledingham, Maydith Wood, Molly Cheyne, Georgina McDonald, ? McIntosh, Annie Leslie, Christine Cheyne, Betty Will. **Front:** Billy Taylor, Arthur Gray, Margaret Leggat, Maisie McIntosh, Rosie Cheyne, unknown, Gladys McGowan, unknown, ? Will, Susan Ledingham, Billy Cheyne, unknown.

Fundraising and thrift

Funds had to be raised to help cover the costs of the meals, and for Christmas, picnics and special occasions. The school funds committee held concerts, dances or whist drives as the need arose.

Some of the children made regular collections round the district for the SPCC and Earl Haig's Fund; the names of the collectors and the amounts collected were noted in the BANFFSHIRE JOURNAL. They also made calendars in December 1936 to be sold in aid of the new Aberdeen Infirmary.

Miss Gray attended national savings conferences in 1932 and 1933. When the WRI held a meeting on thrift in September 1932, the BANFFSHIRE JOURNAL reported the presentation of the subject given by pupils.

A more practical education?

The centenary of Sir Walter Scott's death was marked in school, as reported in the BANFFSHIRE JOURNAL.

'A short Burns programme, including Burns songs and recitations, was given by the children to a number of parents and

FINTRY SCHOOL.—The Scott centenary was celebrated at Fintry on Wednesday. Rev. W. and Mrs Logan, Turriff, visited the school, when Mr Logan gave an address to children, parents and friends in the locality, on Sir Walter. The children gave a programme of Scott's songs and poems. Songs were given by the senior division, solos by Annie Mair; selections from "The Lady of the Lake," by Margaret Ledingham; from "The Lay of the Last Minstrel," by David Henry, and from "Marmion," by Peggy Lorimer, Peggy Thompson, Christina Cheyne, James Ironside and James Rodger. Miss Buchan, headmistress, thanked Mr Logan for his splendid address. He had made, she said Scott and his works a living and interesting subject, and given all of them an impetus to read his books. Mrs Logan thanked the teachers and the children for their admirable programme.

THRIFT.—Fintry W.R.I. met on Thursday, Mrs Ledingham presiding. Mrs Burnett, Methlick, gave a demonstration on Thrift and her introduction of the subject was novel. Margaret Ledingham, Kathleen M'Gowan, Susan Ledingham, Isobel Ledingham, Annie Leslie, Molly Cheyne, Caroline Leggat, Lily Leslie, Peggy Thomson, Christina Cheyne, Margaret Leggat, Annie Mair, Betty Dingwall, Peggy Lorimer, Norman Leggat, Harry Lorimer and David Hendry all repeated little verses describing the thrift articles which they proudly displayed. Mrs Burnett showed by articles she herself made that thrift can be made to work wonders in the home. "It's the littles that

Scott Centenary and Thrift, September 1932 *Banffshire Journal friends who were invited to be present'* in January 1932, and in 1934 six senior pupils wrote essays to compete in the Bon Accord Burns Essay Competition.

Nature study rambles to Craigston Castle became part of the summer term. Much handwork was done, with displays at prize-giving. Prizes were awarded for colouring, sewing, handwork, nature study, writing and music as well as for class work.

The children entered competitions for drawing, the best jotter and named twigs in the Turriff Industrial Exhibition's extensive juvenile section in March 1932. The school took part in SPCA essay competitions regularly, with various pupils winning prizes. The WRI gave spring bulbs for the children to plant and grow for their competitions.

No more advanced division

HMI reports of the early 1930s had shown the difficulties of trying to provide post-primary education in a small school, although it was recognised that *'the results of instructions are quite creditable in the circumstances'*. April 1937 therefore saw the end of Fintry's advanced division, and pupils were sent to Turriff or King Edward schools on the basis of their qualifying exam results.

Empire Day in the 1930s

The celebration of Empire Day was compulsory for all the Turriff area schools in 1934, when it could encourage children in good morals, manners and behaviour. Maj. Ledingham brought along his wireless set so that they could listen to Admiral Jellicoe's talk to schoolchildren in 1933.

In 1937, as Col. Ledingham, he returned to tell the children about his experience of attending George VI's coronation.

The following year Mr Leggat gave a talk to encourage good conduct in home and school so that the children might become good citizens of the Empire.

Outings and events

An annual picnic visited Banff Links in 1932, Sandend in 1934, and Banff again in 1938.

Two royal weddings, George V's Silver Jubilee and George VI's coronation were celebrated with holidays,

Fintry School after 1907, in the 1930s

cinema outings and gifts:

To celebrate the coronation, on Tuesday afternoon the children have the secretary of state's letter read to them, and the coronation explained. Thereafter they receive the medals presented by the county council, coronation mugs given by Mr Buchan, Schoolhouse, and the infants, who do not get to the cinema entertainment in Turriff, receive balls and sweets.

On Wednesday a picnic is to be held in a field near the school, and on Thursday the older children are to be taken to a cinema entertainment in Turriff. (Log Book)

The school in wartime

Evacuees

On 5 February 1940 the log book of the Kent Road Public School in Finnieston, Glasgow recorded the names of the 12 pupils still at Fintry, out of the original 35 evacuated there in September 1939: Kenneth Gillespie; George, Robert and Helen Liddell; Robert Muir; Robert, Esther and Isobel Ross; Jane Geddes; Helen Gibson (Agnes Bolwell's older sister); Janet Noakes, and Frederica Stanley.

Donald and Molly Edwards, relatives of the Ledingham family, from Gravesend in Kent, came as private evacuees. Other private evacuees came from Fraserburgh and Aberdeen and stayed for varying periods. Some 'boarded-out' children came later from the Glasgow area.

The initial influx of Glasgow children added to Fintry's 59 pupils made a double-shift system necessary, but by the end of September, only 27 evacuees remained. Seats were supplied for the cooking room and Miss McLaren, the remaining Glasgow teacher, taught Primaries 2 and 3 there.

As evacuee numbers dropped to 16 by December, Miss McLaren was recalled to Glasgow, and all the scholars were again taught in the two classrooms, with Miss Buchan taking the four senior classes and Miss Youngson the three younger groups.

Kent Road School, Glasgow

Emergency measures

School hours were adjusted to allow work to be completed in daylight, and the teachers put anti- splinter *'lace'* on all the windows. Gas-mask drills took place, with Police Sergeant Cruickshank visiting occasionally to check and replace the masks, and the pupils practised the use of the stirrup pump as part of their fire drill. The volume of military traffic meant that the children had instruction in road safety from January 1942.

Because of the double shift, it was thought 'out of the question' on 13 November to provide hot meals, but two weeks later, with the whole school on a single shift, hot dinners were resumed. The committee also agreed to have the usual Christmas tree with gifts for the evacuees also.

Helping the war effort

Local holidays were not always observed, and the summer vacation was shortened to four weeks in July, with a further break taken to suit the local farmers. Children over 12 were asked to volunteer for the grain and potato harvests, as work of 'grave national importance', so some Fintry pupils helped every year. The education committee minutes of December 1943 noted the Government's thanks for all the help given by the schools in securing that year's harvest.

Fintry children carried out annual house-to-house collections for the Red Cross, the newly formed Blood Transfusion Service, the Earl Haig Fund and the SPCC. They also collected 3575¼ lbs. of waste paper in May and June 1942.

The annual prize-giving in March or early April was usually linked with a sale of work made by pupils and parents for the Prisoner of War Fund. The 1944 effort was particularly noteworthy:

> *Lady Diana Buchan, Auchmacoy House, opened a sale at Fintry School which resulted in the magnificent sum of £233 16s being handed over to the Prisoner of War Fund. In her remarks Lady Buchan gave some interesting information as to how Red Cross parcels reach our prisoners.*
>
> *Fintry was a veritable hive of industry. The school children sold cut flowers, made toys and rugs – one boy alone made 17 rugs. The enthusiasm of the children can be gauged by the fact that they even gave up their pets for lottery. The women made aprons, sewing and knitting bags, stuffed toys and dolls from odds and ends. Not wishing to be left out of the effort the menfolk organised a dance which helped greatly to augment the funds.*
>
> *Fintry School from a similar effort last year made a donation of*

£100 to the Fund. This remarkable achievement on the part of a small country school reflects great credit on Miss Buchan, organiser of the sale, on her pupils, and all who helped to make the event such an outstanding success. (BANFFSHIRE JOURNAL, 25 April 1944)

A total of £419 was handed over by the school to the fund during the war. In 1945, the £159 raised was shared between school funds, the Red Cross and the Turriff and King Edward Welcome Home Funds.

Some light relief

The annual picnic at Craigston Castle continued, and Christmas parties on a limited scale. The travelling film unit visited school in December 1939, and the children attended a Children's Theatre performance in Turriff in May 1940 and a concert given by a group of Dr Barnardo's boys in aid of their own funds in April 1944. The pupils themselves organised the programme and tea for a party on the closing afternoon of the spring term 1945.

They served their country

Fintry lost some former pupils in the war. Norman, only son of Major and Mrs Leggat of Yonderton, died of pneumonia in North Africa. *'He died quite suddenly. He'd still been on the go, and some of his friends thought he should see the doctor, and I suppose he maybe didn't live twenty-four hours after that.'* (Information from Frances Towler)

James, only son of Mr and Mrs Ironside of Mill of Fintry, *'was in the Navy, he was a Radio Officer, he was torpedoed twice, and the third time he didn't survive. And that was their only child.'* (Frances Towler)

There were also two brothers, Peter and Ronald Cheyne, the sons of a farm labourer at Upper Cotburn, who died serving with the Scots Guards.

(James Cheyne, no relation)

Several serving former pupils came through the war safely. Charlie Cheyne was rescued from Dunkirk after three days on the beaches, and also served in Burma. George Arthur Gray served in the navy. James Cheyne, Charlie's younger brother, a farm labourer at Upper Cotburn, was kept in his position by the *'standstill order'*, but served in the Turriff Home Guard from age 18.

(James Cheyne)

Schooldays 1929–1945

Former pupils whose memories are shared here were the children of farmers, small farmers, crofters and farm servants, and also the daughter of the gardener at Craigston Castle. Agnes Bolwell came as an evacuee in September 1939 and stayed for the rest of her primary schooldays.

Getting to and from school

Caroline Leggat: We always walked. We did have moggins, when it was really bad. These were woollen socks pulled over your boots… to give you a better grip in the snow.

Somebody threw [my hat] in the burn, and you wouldn't go home without your hat, so into the burn. And we'd try and find frog-spawn, and we kirned about in the burn. We got clay for making things, there was a bank where you got clay, and then we could go into the wood, if there was no gamekeeper about, and see what was in the wood, flowers or nuts or berries.

Jean Skene: I feel the kids now miss such a lot, because they all go to school by car, bus or something. We walked, and there was such a lot you learned… just

On the school road: Betty and Dorothy Lorimer with Coreena Cowie, 1940

Miss Youngson and infants 1937: Miss Youngson (infant teacher 1937-1940). **Back:** Frankie Sinclair, Alan Dingwall, unknown, Ronnie McBain, John Ledingham, Norman Cheyne, Billy Cranna. **Middle:** Sandy Forbes, Betty McBain, Helen McDonald, Betty Lorimer, Donald Harper. **Front:** Alex McIntosh, ? Cowie, Gertie Reid, Jean McBain, Jimmy Burr, Joe Simpson.

nature things, things you saw on the roads, ach, just... nature. But I don't suppose any o them knows the names o wild flowers... like fit we did.

Ethel McCurrach: I remember it was quite a long way for a five year old, two and a half miles there and the same back, and my older sister Lilias had to carry me a bit as I was tired walking.

Agnes Bolwell: ...the interesting field of turnips to feed us on our way home at the end of the summer. We were profligate with that farmer's turnips which caused him to complain to the school.

Starting school

William Will: I mind on gaun tae the school and nae being ower happy aboot it, you had to go, there was no turning back, but it was a bittie upsetting for a week or so.

Jean Skene: I remember starting school. I howled and I howled. My sister was in the class up from me, and Miss Buchan wouldna let me sit beside her, and I just broke my heart. I remember that. You got this freedom, you went oot to play... and then you were suddenly shut up in the school. And you'd to be quiet. It's a big shock.

In the classroom

Caroline Leggat: ...the abacus, the bright colours of the beads in this, and you counted on the frame. [Letters were] 'A' for apple, I don't know what 'b' was, 'c' for cat. They were mostly a visual image, and a big square for the letter.

We had reading every day, I think, read a bit, and spelling, and in Miss Buchan's, we had mental arithmetic and that used to be well through a Friday afternoon. We had a sort of quick race round with mental arithmetic and of course we had to learn the times tables just as we went up the school. When we got to seven and eight it was really complicated but it was thorough. You didn't move till you did know it.

We had lovely big maps, and I think I was especially interested in maps... you were supposed to know where places were, the rivers and capitals, and which country they belonged to.

We got to knit from Standard 1, and we maybe made

Seniors 1937: Back: George McNaughton, George Smith, James/George Maitland, Alan Reid, unknown, George Will, Robert Winton. **Middle:** Billy Cheyne, Margaret McBain, Kathleen McGowan, Dorothy/Christine Andrew, Georgie McDonald, Margaret Leggat, Mary Forbes, Frances Leggat, Arthur Gray. **Front:** John Will, ? Will, Margaret Cranna, Gladys Davidson, Christina Cheyne, Betty Ledingham, Margaret Clark, May Smith, Alistair Winton.

a kettle-holder first, then we did a tea-cosy. You knitted two lengths, mine was blue on one side, and I think orange on the other, then you sewed them together and doubled them, and that was a tea-cosy. And somewhere along the line, we were sewing, but the length of material, it was called sparva, it was cotton, and out of this you made maybe a pinafore, and there was an attempt to make a pair of knickers, but I hadn't much material left and by the time the garment was made it would never have gone on to me, but Frances was given this to wear, these red knickers.

We had a lot of handwork, you know, plasticine, and making flowers on twigs, and covering them with silver paper, and... what's that, like tissue paper, there's a name for it, we made decorations with it, and then we used to paint eggshells, on strings, for Christmas. You brought along [eggshell halves], and painted them, and strung them.

She was very keen on handwork, Miss Buchan. There's quite a lot of things made with plasticine. Our drawings were up round the wall. There's single stems of daffodils everywhere, and one great thing was bringing wild flowers. Whoever brought the first one for the season, she had columns drawn, and your name went down, and the flower and the date you brought it, and there was great competition for who brought the first specimen annually.

We learned Robbie Burns' poems, and maybe Charles Murray, and Wordsworth. 'I wandered lonely as a cloud that floats on high o'er vales and hills'. I know Norman had to illustrate that and put it into that exhibition. [Industrial Exhibition in Turriff]

On a fine day, if all was well, Miss Buchan would take us out round her garden, which might have been once a month, it wasn't often. I really enjoyed that, she knew so much about plants. And sometimes, if it was a lovely day outside, she would put some of the bigger boys outside. She'd go out and give them good instructions. I daresay they thought that was great, to get out of the classroom. It really gave them something interesting to do.

Kathleen McGowan: She made us do scrapbooks. I don't

think a lot of children got papers delivered to their house. We had. I got super photographs out of them, so of course I got the best scrapbook. I had different things in it, like swans and things.

Sheila Morrison: We were taken rambles down the road and into Craigston Castle grounds. I loved these rambles. Miss Buchan also made a rockery, in the playground just outside the school door, and we all had our own flowers. I had a giant periwinkle, up at the top. I loved going through her garden. She told you all the flowers and you had to say which was which, also the wild flowers.

Lilias McKenzie: We did this collecting, pressing flowers, and the leaves, but the boys used to bring spawn, from the burn, and they went into glass jars with water and they were put up by this… tall window, and they eventually came into tadpoles. And then they had to go and get some chickweed to feed the tadpoles. I think the tadpoles actually went back into the burn before you went away on holiday, at Eastertime, it would have been. I don't think they got the length of being frogs.

I used to do decoration things for Christmas and that. You used to get the stalks with the ears of corn on it, and save up all your coloured silver paper, from sweetie wrappings and things and you covered each corn thing… they were dust collectors afterwards, but never mind, they were bonny when they were done. And you also did beech twigs, it was when the leaves were gone, and with sealing wax, different coloured sealing wax, you made little flowers with yellow bits for their stamens and green for leaves, and you did that on the stalks, and that was flowers.

William Will: I jist wasna interested in that [history]. Things that happened years and years ago, I just said, what's the point, it's aa past. I couldna see the point. But aince you're older, you see it. I should hae listened faun I was younger. We didna get woodwork. I'd a loved that now. We did aa oor raffia. We used to make photy frames, a lot o things we did wi raffia. But there was anither thing, that was the drill outside, she used to line you aa up, you did sic-an-sic, you do this, you do that, an… You had a coloured band, it was about that width [about two inches] over your shoulder and down. We aa had different colours. That was oor drill, on a Tuesday. We didna get it ilka Tuesday. It was aye ootside, in the playground, the kids' playground, it wasna the big ane [but] round the back.

Jean Skene: Miss Buchan had a book, it was huge, and she used to put it over the tap o the blackboard, and this was all religious pictures, and I thought they were beautiful. I loved that. And she used to give us stories aboot one o these pictures.

Murray Ledingham: That was one thing that Miss Buchan was very good at, learning you to write. You got copybooks and you had to… dark up and light down, or vice versa, I canna remember now. You used to get marks for writing. I used to enjoy my writing. And then your mental arithmetic, she was quite strict about it…

Ethel McCurrach: We had a slate. We did not get paper as it wasted paper, and I was the only one with a slate with wood around, a proper finished-off slate, and I felt quite proud. Sheila got it after I was finished with it. You only needed it for a little while until you could do your figures and your ABC. After that you got a pencil and a little jotter, I suppose. We read from the Janet and John books – "Janet says A for apple" and so on.

Coreena Stephen: We used slates a lot, copy books to practise writing, crayons for drawing and discs of coloured tissue paper rolled up and dipped in Gloy to make parrot collages. When I had to play Bo-peep at the end of my first year my father provided the shepherds' crook and a quantity of recently docked lambs' tails. They were attached to the rears of my flock.

We had a test every Friday. It consisted of ten questions on each of the following: Spelling, Grammar, History and Geography and five on Bible. There were also a few arithmetic sums to do.

Doric in school

Jean Skene: You had to sort of talk, which was rather difficult if you'd never talked in your life, ye ken. You were checked if you said something wrong, right enough. I dinna think it was too bad, you just got on with it, and if you said something wrong, they told you and you changed it.

Agnes Bolwell: The Buchan accent was heard everywhere except in the classroom but by then I'd grown accustomed to it and to being called *'a Glasgow keelie'*.

Rewards and punishment

Caroline Leggat: There was a strap, a terrible invention, and people got the strap for misbehaving, or not having done their homework, or something like that. It wasn't often used, and if it was, it was an awful atmosphere. It had a very sobering effect on, just the folk in general, a low point in the day if the strap was out.

We had to provide something for a medal, I've forgotten what it was, a badge or a brooch. There was a penny in the infants' class, the first room, a penny on a string. Because you got home the penny and you had to polish it.

Kathleen McGowan: Sandy got the strap, he was great tall. Goodness knows what he got it for. He shifted his hand, and it walloped down and hit Miss Buchan's leg. She mastered him in the end, you know.

Frances Towler: She [Miss Buchan] was a guid soul, I aye thought she was a wee bittie feart the bigger anes would take advantage o her, she kept a good eye on folk. I was busy taking scraps, mind yon pages of scraps, I got the tag for that.

There was the big loons, they would hae gaun on till 13 or 14 afore they left, some o them were big boys. If they didna dae as she said, she had to ging roon about the desks. The loons, some of them would hae jist stepped ower the desks so they didna get the pinter at them, ye see. Aye, it was a shame. I've seen her once or twice hae her father come in, Mr Buchan, he aye came in to wind the clock on a Friday, but I hiv seen him once or twice in if thingies got ower much for Miss Buchan, just so a man body was there. Oh the boys werena' coorse, just tricks.

William Will: Them that did the best that week got a… lovely brooch, just for the week. That was for the brightest ones, you see. I can mind I got it for a week, I near drappit doon, I wasna awfy clever at the school, but she says, Billy, you can have the brooch this week. I couldna get ower it, I couldna get hame quick enough to tell…

I can mind on my ain brother, he was sitting,… pitting blotting paper in the inkwell, he put it on the end o his ruler… fly, it hit the roof, Miss Buchan just about lowpit aff o her chair, how she kent it was him I dinna ken. She just came right to him, come out here. He got the strap. It was a black mark.

Spikkin aboot him again, he was doing the Lord's Prayer. *'Our Father, which art in heaven'*, he aye says, *'Our father who chawed the pirn'*, he was just across fae me, Miss Buchan, she must hae twigged, and she creepit up, an… was standing aside him… whack, on the side o the face, a good whack. But that teached him, like, he didna say it again.

Jean Skene: I would say the majority of them… were well-behaved. I remember my brother, he'd been going to get the strap for something, and instead of standing up and taking the strap, he run. And he ran round the room, so Miss Buchan was running after him. That sort of thing you would hae maybe got.

Ethel McCurrach: Cathy Smith was always first and I was second or once I was third. You got a prize for the best pressed flowers, or perfect attendance. I never got that. There was a sewing prize. There were quite a few prizes.

Lunches

Caroline Leggat: It was a slice of bread and syrup for playtime, and dinnertime it might have been two slices, and again syrup, and cocoa, or in the summertime we had a bottle of milk.

Kathleen McGowan: I remember all the pupils coming from the country places. They had the bottles of cocoa; they were all lined up in a row right round the fire… they were kept hot there, cocoa for their lunch.

Jean Skene: Every day it was soup, except for Thursdays and it was bradie day. They were lovely bradies, I can taste them to this day, and you got bradies and cocoa.

Ethel McCurrach: The tattie soup was terrible. I think it was to do with the copper boiler the soup was made in. Tattie soup on Monday, pea soup on Tuesday, broth on

Wednesday, cocoa and a bradie on Thursday and tattie soup again on Friday.

It never varied. Miss Buchan used to say to my Mum that we were the only people who didn't like the soup. It was seemingly the meat that was used. It was wartime and it was rabbits that were shot, and maybe we didn't like the taste of rabbit.

Sheila Morrison: In the summertime it changed. We used to take two slices of bread with us, and they put something, cheese or jam, and you got your cocoa with that.

Ethel McCurrach: Because Mrs Davidson was off ill, I did it. I went into the third room at the back, and you had to melt the margarine because it was very hard. You had to spread the bread with the margarine and cheese or jam, and then you made up the cocoa. I did that and got the pay for it.

You put the cocoa and the sugar and the milk in pails, but you weren't allowed to put in the water. Miss Buchan herself came through and put the water in, but I had to have it boiling for her.

Classrooms and facilities

Caroline Leggat: That third room was used for the dental inspection… I think teeth were pulled on the spot… your parents gave permission, and you had to go through to the dentist, and come back and sit down… and the District Nurses also came and… looked us over,

And of course there were these awful toilets. They were a nightmare, and I believe there was rats there too. But somehow you didn't think about… you didn't go unless you just had to.

Coreena Stephen: The windows were tall, above eye level, and as it was wartime, the glass was crisscrossed with tape. A bare wooden floor and lower walls lined with dark tongue, tongue-and-groove woodwork made the place rather Spartan.

About the teachers

Kathleen McGowan: [Miss Buchan] went to the Scandinavian countries, to Finland… and she took films, and she brought them back and she put them on a screen for us. She was a brilliant teacher, because she

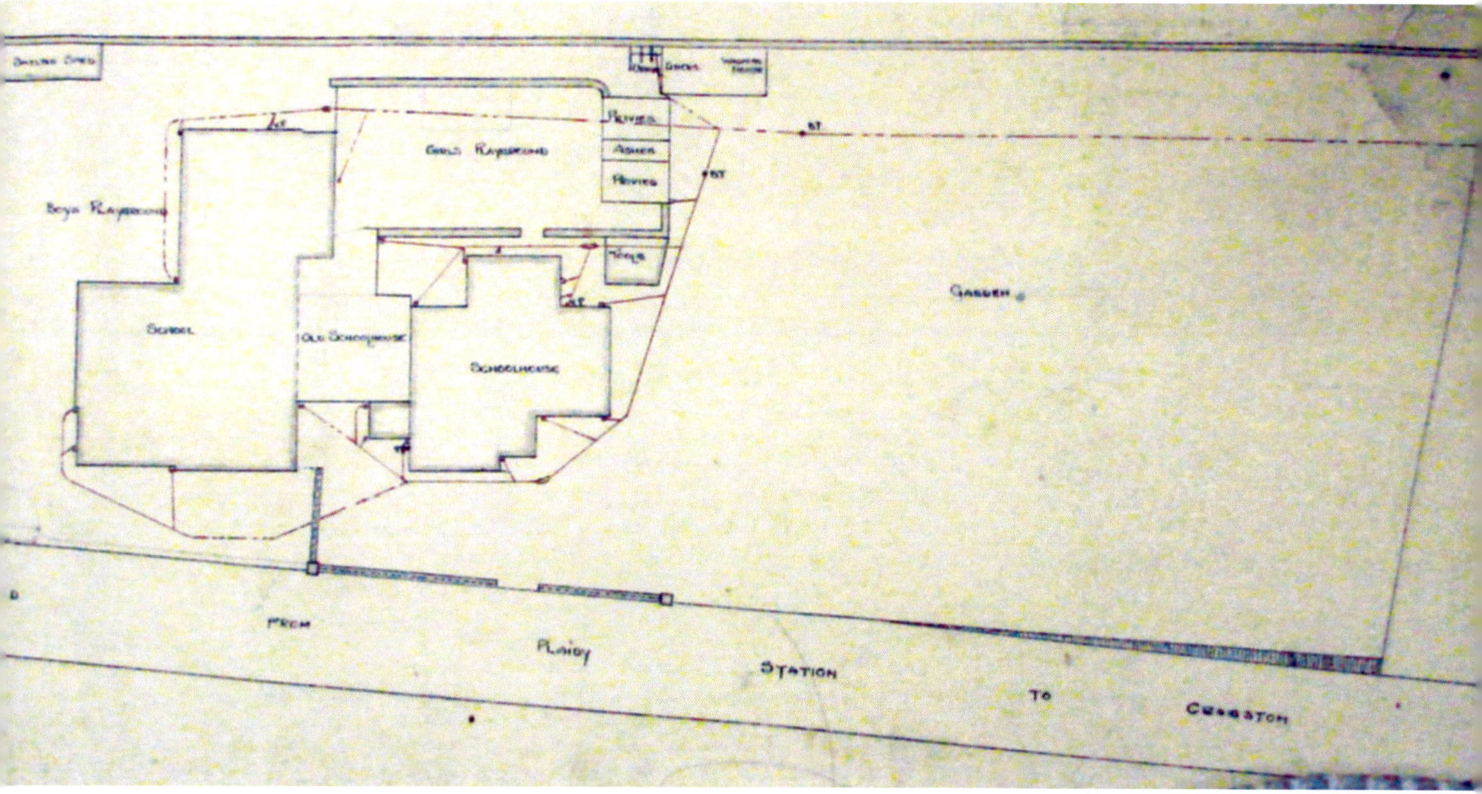

Block plan of school and grounds post-1907

taught us things that nobody else would have known about.

William Will: [Miss Gray] was a lovely teacher… there was very wrong afore she raged you, like. The way she teached you, you never had nae reason to be bad. The only thing I didna like was whiles she'd give you mental, round the class. Oh gee, I was hopeless at it. We had oor books, you had to write between the lines, keep your book neat. She used to read stories. That would have been later on in the day, maybe two o' clock, she'd say, right, I've a story here I'm going to read out to you, and she jist got her book and she'd sit down. Abody was quiet, and you just listened, like. It was stuff like the Three Bears, and that kind of stories that ended up… with somebody being eaten. Red Riding Hood, a that kind of stuff she used to read till's.

Jean Skene: I didn't like the school. From the day I went to the day I left. Miss Youngson was alright. Miss MacLaren was fine. I'm sorry, I didn't like Miss Buchan. I'm sure you won't find a lot o people saying that, but I know I didn't like her. She could be very strict and she used to be mad at times.

Caroline Leggat: The cottars would change, once a year. Most of the married families would only move once a year, or one or two years. And some families came back to Fintry, they'd been there before, and we were so excited to see who was coming after the May term, the new people, to see where they came from.

Community activities

Caroline Leggat: There was services once a month latterly, the minister came from Millseat. There were two ministers, Mr Peace and Mr Laslett, and then the minister came from Turriff, St Andrews', that was Mr Logan originally and there was a lectern put up, and this big Bible. And he had one of these flat hats, you know that picture of the skating minister, well, he looked like that.

William Will: Ony o the concerts or Christmas things that a lot o parents come, they [my parents] niver come to them. We'd a liked to hae seen them there, richt enough… especially if you was in something yersel, you wanted to let them see fit you could dae.

Jean Skene: It was during the war, and we used to have concerts, we used to do concerts for… the prisoners of war, whatever. I'd an elder brother who was a prisoner o war, so… we danced, we sang. I couldna sing. Well, somebody had to sing, a boy and a girl, I had a little nut tree. And there was two of us picked, for a trial to see who could do this. Betty Lorimer and I were picked, and we both sang. And we heard the teachers, they said, she hasn't got such a sweet voice, but she's louder. That was me. So I got this part of singing I had a little nut tree, so I went home and I said, I've got a part, I had a little nut tree. Well, you can't sing. Oh, I can, teacher said I could. Well you can't sing. Just leave it to the other girl. I waited right till the last minute, and I said to the teacher, I'm not doing it, cause I can't sing. So the one with the sweet voice got to do it.

I loved these concerts, and the school was just always packed, nae one night, maybe two nights. And then we used to have sales of work for charity, for forces again. And we used to make all these things for the sales o work, you'd pot-holders, just all these different things. We got old shirts, men's shirts, and we took out the back, and we made aprons, everything was made a use of. Any old clothing like that, it was torn to bits, and made into something else. The shirts, they were lovely, we used to put a binding round the edges.

We got bulbs, hyacinth bulbs, and we planted them in pots and put them in the window, and we'd to look after them, and then some o them were taken to the shows, and I won a prize for my one. And I got two shillings. I managed to buy a jumper with that two shillings.

Christmas celebrations

Caroline Leggat: When it came to the Christmas tree, some of the menfolk helping went round with a long pole and a taper and lit the candles on the tree – live, and when you think of the fire hazard.

There was quite a programme. Previously we'd been practising singing and one or two dances and reciting poetry. We had to practise dancing - the Cumberland

Reel and the Haymakers' Jig. Of course you had to take the boys for partners, or they had to take you, and they weren't keen. Oh we enjoyed it, and it was a great treat from lessons, and Miss Gray would have played for the practices. I suppose it might have been a Friday afternoon, we didn't spend a lot of time practising, but one thing I do recall was making the costumes for some of our dances, for some of our sketches with the crepe paper. On one occasion I was supposed to be the flower, a rose, so I had a green skirt and a red top, and I think put something on our heads, maybe just a band.

I'll never forget Margaret Ledingham reciting The Highwayman. She had her father's army dress jacket and all the trimmings - he was Col. Ledingham – and maybe long boots. I think she could still recite it. We were recalling that at the party *[See Open Day 6 Sept 2011]* and it was quite impressive.

We got prizes off the tree, something for everybody. It was dark except for somebody maybe had a torch, they read out your name and you went and were presented… my last gift was a pink mirror and comb and brush which I treasured.

Frances Towler: Miss Nell Hutcheon was a big, well-built woman, and my goodness, if you didna curtsey, or the loons salute her, look oot, she mentioned it to Miss Buchan. She had these beets, I can see them yet, lang boots with buttons, a stylish kind o woman. She used to come and play for onything. And Bell, Miss Buchan's sister, she was a matron doon in Johnstone, it might have been her holidays, if there was onything like Christmas or Easter, and ony o the bairns that didna manage to gang hame at dinnertime, to dress for the efterneen do, Bell would come in and maybe tidy them up a bittie. She would wash their faces and get their hair deen, oh it was aye great excitement, even afore, making thon paper chines and that.

William Will: There was groups singing… Christmas… carols, there was Jimmy Barron and masel, there would hae been about 12, I think. Miss Hutcheon's coming tomorrow, some of us sat doon an sang along wi her ...but I aye mind she had a black coat, a big fur roon her neck. We used to hae a good gander round the tree, the toys fit we was getting aff the tree was numbered,… and we'd hae a look to see fit oor ain number was. [Santa] was Mr Ledingham again. We knew it was him, but he had on Santy's robes, his hat, and we was a sitting, the teachers said, not a noise, keep quiet, Santa'll be at any time. Bang, bang, bang, [does knocking action], he came in, ho, ho, ho, ho. We were sitting there excited.

Jean Skene: There was a present for everyone on the tree. They were all numbered, and… you picked out of a hat or something. Now I remember this year I picked number one, and they were all saying to me, oh you've got number one, that's the fairy from the top o the tree, and you've to kiss Santa Claus to get it. I was just miserable the whole day. I didn't want to kiss Santa Claus… I got the fairy from the top of the tree, and I didn't have to kiss Santa. I scuttled up and scuttled back. We'd lovely parties. We used to decorate all the school, put up all the decorations.

Agnes Bolwell: My sister and I used to practise all our hymn tunes till we were word perfect and note perfect. To my amazement I discovered that not everyone could carry a tune. Then Miss Buchan broke the news that we were to form a school choir and sing a few carols for the Christmas evening. Parents, guardians and friends and sometimes members of the Women's Rural Institute combined to make this a notable event. Sausage rolls or 'bridies' with hot cocoa were provided and excitement grew as the main classroom was decked with holly and Christmas decorations. These were thick ropes of green and red paper interspersed with the odd holly bough all put up by the boys.

Empire Day daisies

Caroline Leggat: We wore these white and red daisies, I don't know what you call them, but the cattleman's wife had them in her garden… and you put them in your buttonhole. We were very conscious of the Empire, red on the maps on the wall. We were so proud of the Empire.

Picnics and outings

Caroline Leggat: We had a picnic down to Craigston to

the grounds, the Craigston family weren't there. In the bit called the pea fold, there was a steep hill and a flat area beside the burn. We would run races, and we had games, and then there was a bag of eats which was a great treat. I think there would have been a cream cookie amongst other things, and we'd races, sack races, a straightforward race, egg-and-spoon.

Sheila Morrison: There was always a mothers' race, not a fathers'. They were working, or away at the war.

Kathleen McGowan: I remember going to Sandend... and there was a boat sitting in the harbour, and I said to this man, could you take us out in this boat. He said, 'Well, it's not arranged', but I said I'd like to go out in the boat, so four of us went out, away out to sea, and he rowed the boat, and that was at a picnic at Sandend.

Caroline Leggat: We went to Castleton, the farm on the main road, and we walked, of course, from school, and it was a Mr Runciman the farmer, who wasn't married, but his housekeeper provided food for us, probably milk and pieces of some kind, so that was a great joy, we didn't expect it. And there was lots of interest there, we saw round the ruins of King Edward Castle, although the only bit I really remember was the bit that you can see from the road. But we thought that was a great day out. Of course we had to walk back to Fintry, and be dismissed and then walk home.

Wartime and evacuees

William Will: Things changed a bittie again, at the time of the war; there was a lot of Glasgow kids came up here. Upper Cotburn, the next farm to us, they had two, Kenneth Gillespie and Robert Muir, they were about our age, they were great. They stayed... about three, four years? Not to the end of the war... they were really needing hame. They mixed in wi us nae bother, a different way of speaking.

Coreena Stephen: My parents got one boy... he was delivered about 11pm. My mother thought he might be around 8 years old and that he didn't look particularly cared for. She had water ready to give the weary traveller a bath... it became clear he had brought some '*passengers*' with him. The only thing she had was paraffin, so she rubbed his scalp with that. Poor kid! She discovered the next morning that he was 11 years old.

It became common knowledge in the area that one of the [evacuee] boys had *'sorted out'* the school bully. He'd chased him down to the Fintry burn and kept him standing in the water for all of a lunch break.

Another thing which has stuck in my memory is the image of the infant teacher appearing in the connecting doorway. She was in a distraught state and her hair was in wild disarray. Rumour had it that her brother had been killed at the front.

Jean Skene: The first was, there was ever such a lot of them came, boys, girls, all different ages, and they were all out to the farms and people who had room to put them up. And half o them didn't stay. Half o them went right back. And they were all lousy. Oh me, they were lousy, they had to be de-loosed and all the rest of it. But no, there was some nice girls amongst them. There was quite a few that you got friendly with. Some o them stayed till the end o the war, but the majority... they were absolutely lost, there was no chip shop.

I remember one o the evacuees, she stayed round... Craigston way, and she walked to Turriff to get chips. It was dark, and she come back, and just up from our house, there's a sharp corner, and there was a lorry dropped a barrel of black treacle, and she fell in it. She came down to the house, mother tried to tidy her up, and let her get home. What a mess she was in. She didn't stay, she went home. She'd had enough.

Agnes Bolwell: [We] evacuees filled the school to overflowing so seating became something of a problem. At the beginning a Glasgow teacher assisted, a tall very smartly dressed woman who taught us all how to relax. She did this to such good effect that the class joker fell deeply asleep on our very first lesson and fell on the floor. We of course all giggled, which is exactly what Charlie was aiming for. But I had little to giggle about as I discovered that first day. I couldn't do cursive script. Not that I was expected to do it, just that I should be able to read it off the blackboard and then print it out neatly... I had to wait for someone to finish their copy and then lend it to me.

William Will: You had your gas masks sitting in the box beside you, and she'd jist say, *"Right, we're going to have some gas mask drill today. Everybody got a gas mask?"* When she said go, you had to grab your box, get it open, get your mask on and doon aneth the desk, as quickly as you could.

We used to hae to make squares, blankets for the sodgers. Aye, abody was knitting squares.

Sheila Morrison: There were a lot of snowdrops at Craigston, and we used to pick them, and they went to the hospitals for the soldiers. The people who were near Craigston did this, the older pupils, after school or on a Sunday afternoon. The Urquharts from Craigston would phone Miss Buchan and say the snowdrops were ready for picking.

Ethel McCurrach: You had to put them in bundles, and a bit of periwinkle in each, it was the only green that was out then. We tied them up with raffia. That went on for weeks. We knitted scarves too, for the soldiers, in khaki. You thought it was long enough, and she always said you had to knit some more. Boring!

Murray Ledingham: We'd to go round getting rosehips for rosehip syrup. And snowdrops and daffodils, and we used to put them into bunches.

Sheila Morrison: At home we used to collect sphagnum moss and dry it. It was good for wounds. We dried it up in the loft. That was probably through the school as well. We collected paper as well.

Ethel McCurrach: Your schoolbag was on your back, you had to carry your gas mask, then you had papers to carry, then you had carrots, and you were only little and you got weighed down. You wouldn't have had carrots and papers on the same day, mother would see to that.

Playground and play

Caroline Leggat: There was a hole in the ground that was the kypie, and you tried to knock the other balls out and get your ball into the hole. We called it 'bools', marbles. Also *One, two, three a-learie, I saw Mrs Peerie, sitting on a basket cheerie, eating chocolate babies* [was played bouncing a ball against the wall]

William Will: There was the dollar, the bigger ones

[slightly bigger than a 50p piece]. Some o them was stone, some o them was glass. These we actually played wi was jist little lads,... an we jist rolled the dollar first, and where it stopped, somebody gaed up and made a hole wi the heel o their boot, turned roon and roon and roon, till you got a thing like a bird's nest, then we started to roll the little anes an see fa wis near, nearest til't, and some went in it, like, and whoever went in and was nearest claimed the bools. If there was one nearer than ony o the rest, that was aa you got, one. If there was one went in, fair enough, if there was three... Oh, it was great.

They used to tie the ropes on your arms, you was the horse, wi a ploo, that was ane o the farming games. They'd say, fit are ye daein the day? Oh, I dinna ken. Are ye plooin? No, I'm nae plooin. They used to walk along like a horse. Somebody else had the reins at the ither end, keeping you right.

The big playground was big enough. The wee ones had a fair-sized one, they were through fae us, but the girls in oor classes, they didna nae a shelter or naething, they just had to go to the lobby if it was raining, but they were nae allowed in unless it was raining. But we'd a big play green, we did, fae the road richt back to the shelter sheds. As I say, there was aye something to play at, fitiver. You'd get somebody on o yer back and ran roon the place.

Nae in the classroom, mostly playtime, somebody'd take a basin o water outside, come on an dook for aipples... if you were pitting your heid in among the watter, there wis aye somebody ready to... push your heid in. It was great fun to them.

Jean Skene: There's *Fly away, Peter, /fly away Paul, /come back Peter, /come back Paul*... you skipped out and in. There was two at the rope, and one in the centre, and... it was *In comes Peter, /in comes Paul* and you'd two people went in, and *Out goes Peter, /out goes Paul* and both went out and the next two came in.

I think it was more the spring, when the fine days began to come in, you played with the balls... and then the skipping and everything came in. they just seemed to hae their times for playing these things.

We [girls and boys] were kept separate, but always managed that, to throw snowballs.

Snowballs, slides and… just in the playground, where somebody was going to slip. There was no consideration about whether somebody was going to fall or not.

Agnes Bolwell: The playground was plain dirt and pebbles, great stuff when marking out hop scotch beds or 'building' houses. Well, we did after all have little low walls shaped by hand. In winter, however, we took shovels to school and built our version of fully furnished igloos with steps up or down as might be required. Miss Buchan was quite impressed by our ingenuity though I sometimes thought that she would have preferred us to spend as much time on our books as we did on our snow houses.

Ethel McCurrach: There was a season for the ball, and a season for skipping, a definite time for playing with the tennis ball against the wall.

Sheila Morrison: We used to play rounders, and hoppin' beddies, as we called them. We weren't supervised in the playground, you just went out and played and then lined up at the door when she blew the whistle; she didn't have a bell.

Murray Ledingham: We weren't allowed to play football at all, it was absolutely banned in the playground, but in spite of that we played. If the ball went into Mr Ironside's fields, we were barred from going there, and there was a dyke on both sides. Somebody had to go in for it, so in my time I usually went in for the ball, and back in the class afterwards, some girl would say, *"Please, Miss Buchan, Murray Ledingham was in Mr Ironside's park".*

"Is that so?" Well, that was the strap again. I constantly was getting the strap.

A new world 1945–1965

Postwar hardships

With food still rationed the log book mentions jam-making, apparently by some of the pupils, for school meals. Sandwich meals commenced, with the children bringing their own bread; cocoa and then soup was supplied as before, but when the cook was ill, the senior girls had her wages divided among them for preparing sandwiches.

Staff shortages meant that when Miss Moir left, she was replaced by students and untrained teachers. The last of these, Miss McBoyle, taught at Fintry until June 1950. When the school cleaner resigned, Miss Buchan's solution was to employ the pupils.

The teachers' union, the Educational Institute of Scotland (EIS), had hoped that schoolchildren would no longer be used for potato harvesting after 1945, but *'in view of the gravity of the world food situation, after review of all possible adult sources of labour including POWs, the SED was reluctantly forced to the conclusion that this year's potato crop cannot be secured without the help of schoolchildren.'* Strict rules were set for the children's welfare and to minimise the loss of schooling. In October 1946, six senior pupils from Fintry took part, but the minimum age was raised to 13 the following year, and Fintry children were no longer eligible.

A paper salvage scheme continued through to the early 1950s when the director of education congratulated Fintry for collecting the fifth highest amount of paper in their group. It took until 1950 for individual desks and chairs to be provided for the senior room, and it was several more years before the Juniors got spare desks from Ardmiddle School.

When Princess Elizabeth married in November 1947, the Secretary of State for Scotland ruled that because of the need for concentrating labour and materials on essential work, school authorities should not purchase souvenirs or make any but the simplest arrangements for entertaining children on this occasion. Fintry pupils made do with a day off.

Welfare

The post-war Children's Act encouraged people like Miss Skinner of Whiterashes Croft to continue her wartime work of providing a home for *'boarded-out'* or fostered children, often from the Glasgow area. She cared for several children who attended Fintry. The Government Milk Service was set up, and Fintry first had two-course meals (delivered from Crudie School) under the national scheme in April 1949; 35 out of the 40 children took these at the start.

The early 1950s had many stormy winters, when pupils might be dismissed early but the school did not close, even though few attended. An emergency meal of tinned meat, Ryvita, cornflakes and cocoa was usually available in those circumstances. The health of the children continued to be monitored by the school medical officers and district nurse Webster from Turriff, with immunisation against polio introduced in 1956.

When free transport to school was provided for children under eight who had more than two miles to travel to school, Mr Rodger of Plaidy Garage was contracted in March 1951 to bring children from Badentyre Cottage to and from school. However, greater prosperity and increasing provision of benefits by the state were balanced by the cessation of National Savings in the school.

The Scottish Council for Research in Education engaged in June 1947 in a country-wide programme of testing pupils born in 1936: five Fintry pupils participated. The 1950 Memorandum on the Primary Curriculum (in Scotland) declared that the nurturing of the whole child was the aim of primary education, with more emphasis on activity and experience-based learning, and more group and individual work. Visiting teachers were introduced, first coming to Fintry, for P.E. and Art, in 1956–7.

Old and new

Miss Buchan's nature rambles continued, for example to the Dummies' Howe and Strocherie Farm garden in May 1952, and the educational visit retained its pre-war popularity. The older pupils first went to His Majesty's Theatre to see *Snow White and the Seven Dwarves* (January 1949) and also to the Turriff production of *Dick Whittington* (1950) and *Bertha Waddell's Children's Theatre* when it came to Turriff in June 1951.

They took a bus tour to places of historical interest in the area in March 1954, viewing the round barrow and long barrow near Fisherie, and the old churchyard and

Parents' Committee, at Banff Links, 1954: Left to right: Col. John Ledingham (Fintry Farm), Mrs. Metcalfe (Gairnieston), Mrs. McIntosh (Craigston), Mrs. Cranna (Fintry Smithy), Sandy Benzie (Gairnieston), Miss Buchan (Head Teacher), Miss Innes (Infant Teacher), Mrs. Glennie (Backhill of Yonderton), George Norrie (Slackadale).

castle at King Edward and Craigston. This was a joint visit with pupils from Fisherie School. A visit to Slackadale Farm in November that year had Mr Norrie telling 20 senior pupils about the rearing of pigs, poultry and cattle and crop rotation. The senior classes saw over Delgatie Castle in May 1957.

The spread of modern communications meant the installation of a telephone in the school in June 1946. A year later a wireless set was installed with loudspeakers in both classrooms. In the autumn, the scholars were doing exercises using the Schools Broadcasting Service's physical education programme. Ministry of Information educational films were supplied to Fintry from 1948, where the pupils could see the work of a country policeman, or life in India or East Africa.

With added emphasis on games and exercise, a much-needed extension to the playground went ahead, with land bought from Slackadale. This grassy playground was opened in September 1949, and the original one was laid to tarmacadam a year later. *(See APPENDIX 5: HMI Report 1950-1)*

Continuation classes resumed in the school when Col. Ledingham joined the Turriff area education sub-committee: a leatherwork evening class enrolled 23 students in 1949. All the classes in the area showed their work in a crafts exhibition in Turriff in March 1950. The Fintry class followed up with an end-of-session party, music supplied by Mrs Norrie and her son George.

The MIA had ceased to exist but the WRI flourished, taking an interest in the school, for example by entertaining the pupils to a Halloween party in Craigston Castle in October 1946, and providing fruit at Christmas. They revived the pre-war interest in drama, using the school for their 1947 performances. These involved very many of the adults in the area and ended with the ever-popular dance.

The parents' committee now included the wives of two farm servants, the blacksmith and a small farmer as well as three *'large'* farmers and the two teachers. Everyone in the community, from small babies to old folk, excepting the farm workers, attended the annual picnic in 1954.

Celebrating the nation

The Festival of Britain in 1951 saw Fintry and 19 other

Aberdeenshire rural schools receive gifts of window-boxes with begonias, then trees for planting around the playfield. For the coronation of Queen Elizabeth in 1953, the school committee bought a Bible for each child, and paid for swings and a seesaw for the playfield. The Rev. Thomas Wark conducted a service in school, and three days' holiday followed.

A community picnic was planned in a field at Yonderton, but inclement weather forced the event in to the barn. All the Fintry children went to King Edward school in December to see the technicolour film, *Elizabeth is Queen*.

Planning a new school

Fintry had not sought to build a hall under the Further Education Scheme because Craigston Castle Community Centre had provided a venue, but when it closed in February 1953, the community formed a Public Hall Committee and started fundraising. By May 1955, over £600 had been added to £500 from the Craigston enterprise, and a site was granted by Col. Ledingham.

The school roll slid downwards from 1945 to 1951, before rising steadily to 1958, when Mr Eric Taylor inherited a school bursting at the seams with 66 pupils. Two assistants were appointed, with the infant classes being taught in the dining-room.

In June 1958, the hall committee approached the education committee suggesting a joint arrangement for the erection of a general purposes room for both school and community. By 1960 they had agreed to contribute half the additional cost.

Col. Ledingham, who had given so much time and energy to Fintry over so many years, and was a driving force behind the proposed hall, sadly did not live to see it. He died in March 1957, aged 59:

> *Highly respected in the community, he was always ready to lend a helping hand for any worthy cause.*
>
> (BANFFSHIRE JOURNAL, 19 March 1957)

Mr George Norrie took his position on the parents' and hall committee and saw through the local effort to achieve the new school.

By 1961, the centralisation of primary education was

being considered, as rolls were again falling. However, Fintry was placed in Category 1, a school *'reasonably certain to be required long-term'*.

The committee had agreed to acquire an area of ground from Slackadale to bring the school site up to the requirements. The national economy was causing delay in educational building projects, so the S.E.D. suggested that a completely new two-teacher school - with a hall for school and community use – would be better value for money. The hall committee guaranteed an increased contribution of £1,725 and half the cost of furniture and equipment for community use.

Plans were approved, and the new school and hall were opened on 1 September 1964. *(See APPENDIX 6: Tenders Accepted for New School, January 1963)*

Postwar memories

Walking to school

Cathella Mitchell: We were the furthest out on that side, but we picked up children on the road down towards school, the Wills came from the top of the hill, and then there was some farm servant children from Cotburn, but there wasna very many of us. We chattered and we had good company on the way home… There werena many cars on the road, it was safe enough.

There was a library in the… we called it the cooking room, and the Miss Hutcheons used to come down and change their books, with their bikes, and then they'd walk home with us, catch us up on the bike and convoy us home to Cotburn and get all the news.

Myra Simmers: Going to Fintry, walking down the road in the company of the Metcalfes, Gladys was the oldest, so [she] would have seen us all right. The smells I remember, the smell of the broom, eating sourocks at the side of the road. The journeys home in tractor and cart if it was raining, really that sticks out… they used to come down in tractor and cart and bales of straw and a tarpaulin over the top and we got taken home.

I remember prisoners of war, Italians I think, and they must have come to work on the farm, by trailer of some sort, and I remember it tipped at the burn between Slackadale and Gairnieston, and they were kind of sitting recovering as we came on them on our way to school. Another thing I do remember being frightened of, low flying aircraft. We would sometimes cross the fields and these planes seemed to be flying, presumably on training exercises.

Janet Byth: A favourite activity was *'carl-doddies'*. We picked wild plantain, and re-fought the 1745 Jacobite Rebellion by hitting each other's flower-head until one stem was broken. 'Carl' was Bonnie Prince Charlie, 'Doddie' was George II.

First days

Maisie Cheyne: I ran off to school when my Mum was in hospital having my brother Sandy. Miss Buchan told my mother I could stay with my two sisters, Jean and Margaret, until my Mum came home out of hospital.

Myra Simmers: I think it was quite difficult because I'd

Fintry seniors 1940s: Back: James Alexander, Ian Imlach, ? Paterson, ? Paterson, unknown, unknown, Ian Anderson. **Middle:** George Metcalfe, Nan Mackintosh, Gladys Metcalfe, Sheila Cruickshank, Ann Singer, Nora Gibson, Margaret Will, George Ogg. **Front:** Jean Simpson, Margaret Macdonald, Lettie Burns, Jean Irvine, Frances Mackintosh, Margaret Grant, Cathella Anderson, Margaret Alexander, Evelyn Balloch.

been an only one and suddenly there were a lot more, boys, and I wasn't used to that. I'd had a sheltered upbringing to that point, not going to nursery school as they do now.

Maxwell Glennie: The first day, one boy came, he was starting as well, he did nothing but cry all day.

In the classroom

Cathella Mitchell: My teacher was a Miss Clark, and she was a quiet, kind lady, reddish haired, neat, wore a lot of green. We sat at a desk, I still had a slate and a slate pencil and I remember practising my letters. The big black stove fire was lovely and you dried your mittens on the guard, and you put your bottle of milk on the top of the grid of the fire to keep it warm for your morning break. I had Miss Moir in the second set of classes. She was lovely, a tall, dark lady, pretty with a 1940s hair style, and she wore a lot of maroon clothes. She kept discipline because I think I got a bit of a row from her once. We used to do our arithmetic or practising our letters and our writing, on lined and squared blue-covered jotters. And the infants had long desks, the seat came up and the sloped top also came up.

Miss Buchan was a different kettle of fish altogether. She seemed to me to be a very old lady, but she was teaching a long time after I left. And she had white hair drawn back into a bun at the back, and sort of solidly dressed, and she kept really good discipline.

We had to read aloud in class… the next person did another bit, a bit more. I think we stood up at the side of our seats and did the reading. I didn't like singing, and if she asked me to sing by myself, I lost my voice. We had a competition every year, for your Burns certificate. I learned *To a Mouse* and *To a Louse.*

We always had prayers in the morning, prayers and a hymn, and teacher played the piano. I was a bit of a chatterbox at school, and I found myself standing quietly behind the blackboard a few times. That was the punishment, if she caught you chattering, not doing your work wrong, but misbehaving.

Our sewing, we made this lovely lap bag, I had it until quite some time ago. And on the afternoons, on a

Fintry Infants with Miss McBoyle, 1946: **Back:** Ian Imlach (Brackens), Sandy Metcalfe (Gairnieston), John Singer (Mill of Fintry), James Wilson (Wellington), Sandy Burr (Lower Cotburn), Miss McBoyle. **Front:** Evelyn Balloch (N. Lodge, Craigston), Gladys Milne (Gairnieston), Helen Beattie (Gairnieston), Maisie McDonald (Fintry Farm), Muriel Metcalfe (Gairnieston), Grace Balloch (N. Lodge, Craigston), Mary Will (Hill of Cotburn), unknown (Wellington?).

fine day in the summer time, she would take us for walks, down the road toward Craigston Castle. And I remember going in the drive and seeing the rhododendrons, and we had to learn all the wayside flowers and everything, and there was also a competition on that, because you pressed the flowers and put them in a book.

In the Infants, the noisy ones or the ones that needed extra help, they were seated at the front. We had a small class.

When we were in our last year, we made a rockery at the end of the playground and we put plants in it. We walked round [Miss Buchan's] garden, and named the plants. There was a plant you called 'leave me alane an I'll cover the stane'.

Queen Victoria and stuff like that; Einstein, and Robbie Burns sticks in my mind. David Livingstone. The guy who went to the South Pole, Scott, we heard about him. Sir Walter Scott, of course, my Mum was quite interested in Sir Walter Scott.

I think the discipline was good… a good basic education in all the ground subjects. Whether it prepared us for later life at that time, I don't know, but we got a good understanding of letters and figures and reading and stuff like that.

[The school] had a telephone installed, in a little cabinet on the wall, and Miss Buchan was very proud of that. And do you know what she did? She went through to the house, and she phoned through, so that we could have a practice on the phone. The first time I'd answered a phone.

Dorothy Morton came from the central belt and she had this different accent and I think we teased her a bit about it. Kids are not very kind, are they?

Maisie Cheyne: Even the Andersons from Litterty did not miss school [in bad weather] and they had a long way to come.

I liked nature study and I won a book for it. I was never good at art, I drew stick men and a house with straight lines, a door and windows. I was quite good at sums and mental arithmetic, the times tables which I still use. I liked geography. We used slates and a skally, a slate

Seniors 1948: Back: Henry Leslie (Findale), John Singer (Mill of Fintry), Ian Wilson (Kinminty), Sandy Metcalfe (Gairnieston). **Middle:** unknown, James Wilson (Wellington), Helen Beattie (Gairnieston), Isobel Leslie (Findale), Maisie McDonald (Fintry Farm), Charles Ure (Crossfields), Douglas Reid (Mill of Craigston). **Front:** Pat Singer (Mill of Fintry), Grace Balloch (N Lodge, Craigston), Margaret Ure/Rose (Crossfields), Ann Smith (Upper Cotburn), Muriel Metcalfe (Gairnieston), Mary Will (Hill of Cotburn), Betty Scorgie (Lower Cotburn).

Seniors 1950: Back row: James Wilson (Wellington), Ian Anderson (Litterty), Henry Anderson, Ian Wilson (Kinminty), John Singer (Mill of Fintry), Sandy Metcalfe (Gairnieston). **Middle row:** Evelyn Balloch (N Lodge, Craigston), Helen Beattie (Gairnieston), Margaret McDonald (Fintry Farm), Nan McIntosh (Mill of Craigston), Lettie Burns (Whiterashes), Cathella Anderson (Litterty), Maisie McDonald (Fintry Farm). **Front:** Muriel Metcalfe (Gairnieston), Elsie Milne (Gairnieston), Mary Will (Hill of Cotburn), Dorothy Pittendreigh (Yonderton), Ann Smith (Upper Cotburn), Grace Balloch (N Lodge, Craigston).

pencil and a cloth to wipe your slate. We had school milk daily. The minister, Mr Wark, came to school, and there was Sunday School every second or third week.

Myra Simmers: I think you were always on edge. I remember somebody being sick in the classroom and that was frowned upon. A boy, it was.

I remember a picture, which hung above the fireplace, of Jesus with little children, and it said underneath, *'Suffer the little children'*. That would have been my first recollection of the Bible.

My mother used to often go down and see [the Misses Buchan] and I remember going back after I'd left, my mother was asked back to do the prize giving. I remember her handing out apples to everybody. That was a treat in those days.

Janet Byth: My first teacher threw the strap across the classroom one day and hit me on the face with it. I sat petrified while one of the boys sitting behind me prodded me in the back and said, *'She wants you'*. However it was him she wanted. There was no apology, and for the rest of that first year I was scared of the teacher. There were only two girls in my year, and five boys. The boys were very lively.

Our next teacher, Miss Innes, was a gentle and enthusiastic lady, who brought out the best in her pupils. There was one little boy in my class who sang to himself all the time. After some time of this, he disappeared from school and my mother told me he had gone to a special school.

We heard Handel's *Largo* on the school gramophone, and for sewing, I had to make a pair of pink knickers with elastic in the waist and legs - I suppose it taught me to do French seams!

There were photographs of former Fintry pupils who had died in the Second World War, and poppies were placed by them every Armistice Day.

My brothers and I had school lunches as we lived too far away to go home. The food came in large heated tins. I remember semolina with raisins, *'spotted dick'*. We took a jam sandwich with us for our playtime 'piece'.

There were very few children's books in the library, which seemed to cater more for the adults in the community.

Miss McBoyle and infant pupils 1950: Back: Miss McBoyle, Sandy MacDonald (Fintry Farm), George Birnie (Gairnieston), unknown, unknown, unknown, James Cooper (Slackadale). **Middle:** Ian Merson (Craigston), Douglas Reid (Mill of Craigston), Kathleen Simpson (Cotburn), Margaret Ure (Crossfields), Charles Ure (Crossfields), Kenneth Will (Hill of Cotburn). **Front:** Oliver Smith (Upper Cotburn), unknown, Janet Glennie (Backhill of Yonderton), Pat Singer (Mill of Fintry), Myra Leggat (Gairnieston), Rosemary Smith (Upper Cotburn), Albert Reid (Mill of Craigston).

Miss Innes and infants 1952: Back: Ian Taylor(?), Sandy Chalmers (Fintry Farm), unknown, George Birnie (Gairnieston), Kenneth Will (Hill of Cotburn), ? Taylor (Yonderton), Tommy Cooper (Slackadale), Miss Innes. **Middle:** unknown, Rosemary Smith (Upper Cotburn), Evelyn Adam (Hill of Barnyards), Janet Glennie (Backhill of Yonderton), Evelyn Cooper (Slackadale), Polly Smith(?) (Craigston). **Front:** Robbie Cooper (Slackadale), unknown, John Glennie (Backhill).

John Glennie: The use of Doric was not encouraged, as at that time it was seen as the language of the uneducated.

Evelyn Strachan: I thoroughly enjoyed my schooldays at Fintry. I would say it helped mould me into the person I am today. We had dancing classes with Mrs Mitchell from Banff and Miss Stuart as pianist.

Maxwell Glennie: We still had slates and chalk to start with [in 1953]. We had some visiting gym teachers; we were taken outside for physical exercises. We did some running, stretching, that type of thing, running races.

I don't think I was bothered about going to school; my older sister and brother were already there. We had art, but it was the class teacher who took it. There was a visiting art teacher as well. Music, we had singing. There was a piano in the school, and cymbals, triangles, tambourines.

We did a bit of Scottish history, geography. I wouldn't say my education was particularly Scottish. I don't think Doric was used in school. It was plain English with a Scottish accent.

Once you were in a seat, you had to stay in that seat throughout term, not dependent on results of tests. There was a star chart, different colours, black, silver and gold, maybe red, possibly in the whole school, definitely in Primary 4, 5, 6, 7.

We might have worked in twos, fours in art, craft, otherwise individually. You had to share the scissors for craft. There was no moving of desks.

John Ledingham: No. I niver enjoyed the school. The teacher once said I was more interested in what was happening outside than I was inside… I learned a lot mair efter I left the school, aboot counting and hundredweights and pounds and kilos. I suppose at that time, if the teachers realised that you wasna awfy interested, they didna seem to worry.

We was asked to do the nine times table. There was only two or three people in the hale room, the hale class, got it right, the rest o us aa got it wrong, so we aa got the strap. The ten times table, the eleven times we didna learn, we was telt to learn the twelve times table, and I come back on the Monday and I knew it by heart, and I still ken it by heart yet. We'd have paid mair attention. I wish I'd got the strap after the two times table, I'd have paid mair attention to the rest o them.

I used to bike home for my lunch every day, I took my sister on the bar of my bike, and I bikit her back and fore as well. If the school was open, you had to go. One occasion the school lunches couldna come from Crudie School, so it was tins of something opened. I wasna allowed hame that day, I had to stay for my lunch, just in case, it must have been blowing snow.

Eric Taylor was a Doric-spoken lad ony wey, and I dinna think it was discouraged. I think I always used it, never really talked …

Andrew Norrie: Eric Taylor [taught] pretty much the three 'R's, Arithmetic in the morning, English in the afternoon, the odd geography, history lesson on radio.

Graeme Benzie: My first prize book was *THE BUTTERCUP FARM FAMILY,* and I still have it.

Fellow pupils

Maxwell Glennie: Most would have come from farming background, either farmers or farm servants. There might have been a blacksmith or joiner, there was no agricultural engineering.

[Incomers] weren't segregated or picked on. I wouldn't say they were bullied. There might have been the odd scrap, but not bullying.

Playground games

Cathella Mitchell: You see we were on a farm and it was great to mix with other kids.

We did skipping with the long rope, and a few of us going in and singing songs, and we did short ropes and everything. We did hopscotch, we did tackie a lot, ball games as well, and we did *'One, two, three a-learie, I saw Johnny Peerie, sitting on a bumbaleerie, eating chocolate babies'*. Then we did *'Eetle, ottle, black bottle, eetle ottle oot'*. And I can't remember the rest, there was other two lines. Then we did bouncing a tennis ball against the wall, and under your leg, things like that. [shows action of putting ball under knee].

Fit wis that we did? *'One potato, two potato, three potato, four'? 'Five potato, six potato, seven potato, more'* [puts one clenched fist above the other]. You did it with two people.

Miss Buchan was quite strict, you got to play in the cloakroom on a rainy day or a cold day, windy days. She came in one day, to go back after lunchtime, I suppose, here's us all in the cloakroom dancing the sword dance. She just nodded and went past. And I was, just, she's going to give us a richt row, but she didna.

John Ledingham: There wasna much room in the old school for games and things. The new school, well there's the swings and there was a fitba pitch. I'm nae sporty-minded, but there was the badminton in the evenings, and the judo. We went to aa that.

Oh aye, we was aye playing farming games. I was combining, I was plooing, whatever was happening at home, was happening in the playground.

Maxwell Glennie: Playtimes, on fine days you got outside. In the morning playtime you got a drink, a small bottle of milk, and then, you didn't have very long, you just ran about.

The dinnertime playtime, you got longer, if there was a ball, you kicked it. Or you played chasies or the likes of Hide and Seek, Cops and Robbers, you had to catch somebody; Cowboys and Indians.

There was a bit of segregation [of boys and girls], up in the field, they might have played in groups, separately.

The first three [classes], Primary 1 to 3, they mainly played in their class groups, they did not really mix with the big ones. The older ones might have been told to look after younger ones.

The main playground had a shelter cum cycle shed at one end, it was a fair size, then up beyond that, there was a small field with concrete steps up to it. There was a big cistern, and swings. The blacksmith made them, I remember.

Alexander Norrie: I do not remember any bullying or swearing. Playground games throughout the year, many having homemade *'props'*, for example *'high heelers'*, using two empty syrup tins on strings which added a noisy five inches to your height! In my time, P.E. or gym on a regular basis was non-existent – however we got plenty exercise in the playground.

Teachers

Maisie Cheyne: Miss McBoyle was lovely, strict, and Miss Buchan was strict. We were friendly with her because we took her milk every day, but she was strict. If you did anything wrong, you got the ruler over the knuckles.

She travelled, she always had something for us when she came home. She brought me a leather pencil-case from Israel. She told us about where she had stayed.

Myra Simmers: Miss McBoyle, she'd been up to the house for her tea. I suppose if she was in digs my mother would have felt sorry for her.

Janet Byth: Miss Buchan's classroom had lots of lovely pictures on the walls: I think they were the famous Shell natural history pictures. She told us about her holidays in South Africa and Table Mountain with its flowers and cable cars.

John Glennie: I, like a lot of other pupils, would have fared better but for the attitude of the headmistress, a harridan who ruled by intimidation and humiliation.

Maxwell Glennie: Miss Innes was friendly, you weren't nervous of her. In the other part of the school, there was Miss Buchan, she was a wee bit fiery, to say the least. I just had her one year, then Eric Taylor. I didn't enjoy school until Eric Taylor.

Andrew Norrie: Bad memory – frozen milk thawed in front of the fire.

Kathleen Reid: I started teaching under Mr Eric Taylor, in the last year of the old school, so conditions were not very good. We still had the old solid fuel fire which I had to re-stoke. The toilets and cloakrooms were very basic. There was not a lot of equipment and books, I had to make jotters from a big roll of newsprint which I sewed together, mainly for P1 to practice writing.

Outings

Cathella Mitchell: I can't remember what I did, the day before, but my punishment was, *'You're not getting to the pantomime tomorrow, you've misbehaved'*. I went home and I said to Mum, crying of course. And pantomime, nobody'd ever been to a pantomime, it was Peter Pan, and my Mum said, *'Well, you jist go doon in the morning,* *here's your good coat, and you'll gang awa to the pantomime'.*

Down I went and the bus came, and I had on my coat, but I was not allowed in to the bus. And they all went off on the bus to the pantomime without me. I had completely forgotten about it until Jean Irvine came over from New Zealand, and she said, *'You know, I had this awful memory of seeing you standing in the playground and the bus going away without you'.*

And do you know what happened? My mother had also been a teacher, and I don't think her relationship with Miss Buchan improved any, because Mum somehow or other got Miss Buchan to take me and a friend in to see that pantomime later on in the Christmas holidays.

Myra Simmers: I remember picnics, to Tarlair and Banff. The beach, the sea, the first time I'd been to them. Going in a bus was an exciting thing to do in those days. You got the picnic when you got there, in a paper baggy. Swings, chute. I was terrified of the chute, I wouldn't go down it.

Janet Byth: In October 1955, I was sent off to Broomlee School Camp in Midlothian near West Linton for a whole month. I enjoyed the experience, meeting pupils from Rothienorman, the Gordon Schools, Huntly, and from the mining village of New Cumnock in Ayrshire. We visited Edinburgh Zoo and the Castle, had lunch in the Minto Hotel in Edinburgh, and sat most of the qualifying exams at the camp.

We lived in wooden dormitory huts, with cold water to wash in every morning. I can't recall any showers or baths but I suppose we must have had some in a whole month! The camp was wooden buildings, set in woodland, very pretty. That month was a highlight of my schooldays.

Maxwell Glennie: They usually found somewhere to take you that it was raining. We got wet, certainly cold! At Banff Links, it was like a sports day, with races. Possibly there were prizes. I don't think I won anything. Sack races, jumping.

We were marched up to Fintry Farm once, for Col. Ledingham's funeral.

Andrew Norrie: School picnics always a good day; each

pupil got sixpence to spend when we got off the bus. Places visited included the Cooper Park, Elgin, Tarlair and Fraserburgh. Can remember the picnic cancelled at Aberdeen Beach because of typhoid.

Celebrations

Maisie Cheyne: At Christmas we had a nativity play, and every year my Dad was Santa and we never knew! He got the afternoon off work from Mr Ledingham to give all the kids a present off the tree. He did it all the time we girls were there. There was the Nativity play, then the party, then Santa.

Janet Byth: On the day King George died, Miss Buchan came through, very upset, to tell Miss Innes and then us of his death and that we now had a queen. As a seven-year-old, I was thrilled until my mother reminded me that the king had died!

When the Coronation came, we all got a blue tin pencil-case with chocolate and an illustrated Bible. Miss Buchan was excited about the conquest of Everest. There was a gathering in the barn of Yonderton Farm, with all the adults and children in the community there, and we were shown cartoon films.

I remember being Cinderella for a Christmas concert, with Sandy Chalmers as Prince Charming. We were taught how to dance a minuet for it.

Andrew Norrie: Christmas parties were great, with a parcel for every child on the big tree and Santa's visit. My grandmother played the piano for the games.

The community around the school

Maisie Cheyne: I remember my parents dressing to go to whist drives, plays, and Mum went to evening classes in basket-making.

George Norrie: Maybe the WRI had a whist drive, there was sales of work and things like that, so there was always something to do at the school. We were expected to go in to Turriff and take oot 24 card tables for the whist drive, and see to getting the school all prepared for that, on the Friday night, and cart everything back on the Saturday.

It's a country district, Fintry, and they depended on

Burns Supper 1956: Left to right: Janet Glennie, Frances Leggat, George Norrie, George Gill, Col. John Ledingham, Peggy Wilson, Jean Norrie, Madge Anderson.

the support o the farmers, and others, of course, but the farmers in general, they gave a lot of support to the community. Everybody in the district who had children at school readily supported the activities at school.

A whist drive and dance was the usual activity, on a Friday night. We didna go to any great extravagance with expensive bands. Nowadays musicians are quite well rewarded, and you think that we used to maybe get a three-piece band for £4.50.

Jean Norrie: Once a month, on a Sunday afternoon, we used to have a religious service in school. We usually [attended], and once we had family they were encouraged to go, although occasionally they were a bit unwilling and ran off to their other grandparents, but were rescued and taken back to go to the service. The local minister from Turriff was invited out and he would have his afternoon tea at Yonderton, and Mr Leggat would take him back. We felt… we'd been to the church in the morning, we grown-ups werena just all that enthusiastic, but Miss Buchan wanted the service at the school.

Janet Byth: I remember going to whist drives, also a barn dance in the farm loft at Fintry Farm, and a Burns Supper in school. I was the only girl in P7, so I was asked to present a gift to the man who gave the Immortal Memory.

Building the new school

George Norrie: Our community club gave a donation to the education authority and that was used to make the general purposes room significantly bigger to make it into a community hall.

John Ledingham: I remember raising money for the new school. The thing that I remember was a box full of sand, and you put in your pin, to find buried treasure, and you won something.

In the new school

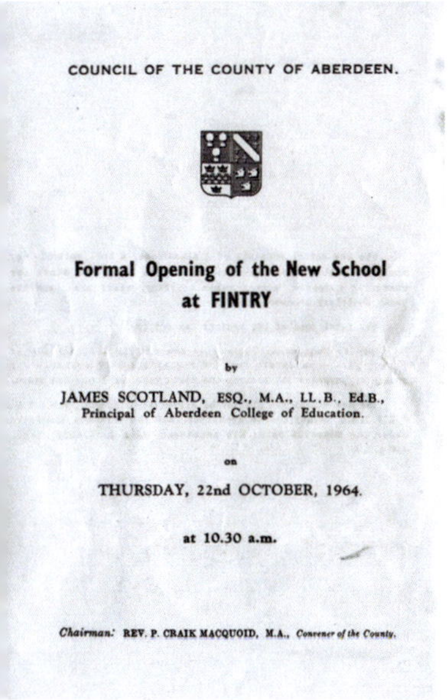

COUNCIL OF THE COUNTY OF ABERDEEN.

Formal Opening of the New School
at FINTRY

by

JAMES SCOTLAND, ESQ., M.A., LL.B., Ed.B.,
Principal of Aberdeen College of Education.

on

THURSDAY, 22nd OCTOBER, 1964.

at 10.30 a.m.

Chairman: REV. P. CRAIK MACQUOID, M.A., *Convener of the County.*

When James Scotland, Principal of Aberdeen College of Education, carried out the official opening of the new school, he spoke of the importance of primary schools in keeping the community spirit alive. He referred to the Community Club and thought its activities brought an awareness of community to the children through their parents' participation.

A BBC TV camera crew came to film the children at work in the modern premises for a programme on education for *'Talk of the North'* in March 1965, and on another occasion, Mr Harper, the BBC Schools Liaison Officer, came to observe while the children listened to an *'Exploring Scotland'* broadcast.

The opening of the new school coincided with the publication of the Memorandum on Primary Education in Scotland. The principle that education should be *'based on the needs and interests of the child and the nature of the world in which he is growing up'* underlay the new approach and took cognisance of the development of mass communications, social change, and increased leisure in the mid twentieth century.

'Language Arts' replaced spoken and written English and *'Environmental Studies'* brought together history and geography, mathematics, science and nature study. Learning would progress at the child's pace, responding to the child's curiosity and desire to learn. Classrooms would be arranged to provide areas where pupils could work together in research and practical learning, and the school day was to comprise a blend of structured learning, art and craft and other recreative activities, and free play.

The new methods were not immediately approved; a meeting of local primary headmasters and teachers at Fyvie in 1967 expressed the view that the new method of the child finding things out for himself is *'going to make their* [the teachers'] *position far more difficult'*.

New theory in practice

James Findlay occupied a building well-suited to the modern methods, and the school progressed towards the new curriculum with the aid of visiting teachers, for P.E., art, music and homecraft/needlework.

Many in-service courses helped the teachers adjust to the new curriculum; these covered topics such as arts and crafts, physical training, numbers, decimalisation and metrication. The qualifying exam was replaced with verbal reasoning, English and arithmetic attainment tests in Primaries 6 and 7. By 1975 the reading lab system was in use for the seniors.

The traditional prize-giving was dropped after 1966; thereafter an open evening was held in June, which displayed the children's classroom work, vocal and instrumental music, and some drama.

The education committee's policy for the arts led to more emphasis on drama, with Primary 5, 6 and 7 pupils attending a Theatre Centre Limited presentation in September 1970. This charitable group, supported by the Arts Council of Great Britain, aimed to help schools develop drama.

Aberdeenshire had its own games, sports and outdoor activities committee to encourage sports among schoolchildren and others. Fintry's new large playing field hosted teams from Crudie and King Edward from 1967 for three-school sports: Fintry eventually had a decisive win in 1972, with only 22 pupils out of the 123 children and teachers who took part.

The school also took part in wider inter-school sports at Monquhitter from 1971, and after the Turriff community swimming pool was opened in 1973, the Fintry children had weekly lessons there, eventually sharing the lessons with King Edward School. Visits were made to a *'Safety in Adventure'* exhibition and to Aberdeen Art Gallery in 1972.

The senior pupils made visits to Huntly telephone exchange in 1967 and Aberdeen harbour in 1970 - possibly linked with project work - and the 1971 picnic to Peterhead Lido Beach included a tour of Kirkburn Mills. The picnic had by this time gone upmarket with high tea in a hotel.

Environmental studies included a talk from Insp. Taylor of the Aberdeen SPCA on the effects of oil pollution from the Torrey Canyon on animals and birds. The 1970s brought new Health and Hygiene courses, National Cycling Proficiency classes, and the introduction of the Green Cross Code and the Tufty Club for road safety. A parents' evening in June 1969 helped to familiarise parents with the coming change from imperial to metric measures.

Judo, badminton and bowling clubs were set up to use the new hall, in addition to the WRI and some further education classes. A branch of the county library continued in the new school. When the government stopped the supply of free milk to schoolchildren over seven in 1971, and only five-year old Kenneth Cheyne in the school qualified for free milk, the committee bought five pints daily for all the children to share.

Threat of closure

By early 1971, pupil numbers had fallen to 21 and on Mr Findlay's departure, an interim appointment was made, for a one-teacher unit. A survey of the provision of primary education in Aberdeenshire was declaring that three-teacher units should be the smallest primary schools in the county. The Fintry roll fell to 15 in August 1973, but the school was not under immediate threat, until a new primary and nursery school in Turriff might be built.

In the event, there was such widespread opposition to the proposal to close 23 rural primaries initially and possibly 20 more, that the scheme was put on hold, to await the new Grampian regional authority and population growth forecasts. By 1974, with numbers still only at 21, Mrs Catriona Tawse was appointed head teacher with Mrs Sheena McHattie joining her in October as infant teacher.

Around 1980 Grampian Regional Council closed Ardmiddle School and some other rural and city schools, but delays in building the new Markethill school in Turriff and the need for nursery accommodation there in the early 1990s ensured Fintry's survival, especially as numbers rose steadily to 36 by August 1993.

Extra help for teachers

The region's Advisory Service was set up in 1975 with 43 Advisers who paid regular visits to the schools. Educational psychologists were on hand too to help pupils, and remedial teaching became learning support by 1987.

When corporal punishment was finally abolished in primary schools in 1984, new strategies were required for discipline, and Mrs Findlay attended a course on behaviour problems in 1992. In-service and Head Teacher Association meetings discussed multi-cultural education, racial tolerance and child abuse as the 1990s progressed.

From 1980 a school closure of eight hours per session was allowed for in-service training. The head teachers spent much time away from school attending sessions on all aspects of education and school management. Fintry hosted two days' in-service training on assessment in April 1988 when Mr Douglas Paterson, Primary adviser, *'spoke on assessment as he sees it and gave an example of good practice.'*

Because of the frequent absences of head teachers, relief teachers became a regular presence in the schools. When Mrs Helen Findlay became head teacher in August 1982, her first entry in the log gives the staff at that time:

Mrs Sheena McHattie, Infant Teacher, Visiting Teachers Douglas Watt (Music), Mrs Roslyn Corbett (Remedial), Mrs Sheena Forsyth (Gym), Mrs Violet Milne (Homecraft), Mrs Doreen Mair (Head Teacher Relief), Mrs Susan Gray (School Secretary, Friday mornings) and Mr Bain, King Edward Church (School Chaplain).

After new conditions of service for teachers came into effect in 1988, planned activity time was introduced, with the Fintry teaching staff spending one afternoon a week from 3.40–5.10PM throughout the school year planning and preparing lessons together. Lunchtime supervisors and clerical assistance became the norm.

And for pupils

Increasing concern for the emotional development of young children meant more liaison with pre-schoolers, secondary school, parents and other rural schools. The teachers spent time meeting pre-school children and their parents, bringing them in to school for a half-day weekly, even letting them try out school lunches in June 1991.

The Primary 7 pupils spent two days at Turriff Academy the same month to accustom them to the senior school. In previous years they had merely had visits from Academy teachers to tell them what to expect. An exchange day with

Markethill Primary in Turriff (20 May 1987) gave the younger pupils from both schools a taste of town or country schooling.

Smaller rural schools cooperated in annual inter-school sports and swimming galas, and in the Inter-School Quiz to *'develop strong communication ties between the five schools – Crudie, King Edward, Fintry, Greeness and New Byth'*. Fintry won at least twice, in 1983 and 1984.

Beyond the classroom

The new methods required research resources for the children to use in school. The Schools Museum Service ensured that a collection of artefacts was available. Scots language and culture were promoted, and the infants were taken to the Festival of Doric at Fyvie School in 1976.

In Mrs Tawse's time, the senior pupils went as far afield as Skye, as part of a farming/crofting project, and to Edderton, Tain, where they took part in a Saturday morning drama class, visited a cheese factory and a museum, saw round a distillery and viewed the graving dock at Nigg Ferry. In due course these outings became more local, visiting Fraserburgh, Macduff and Banff, and Alford Transport Museum, but farther afield to Culloden in 1984.

The whole school went by bus in June 1983 to Inverurie and boarded a train for Aberdeen where they were shown round the railway station. After a picnic in the Duthie Park, they had a conducted tour of Aberdeen Airport and a *'quick visit to an aeroplane'*. In 1986 the infant classes visited the Turriff Heritage Cottage Museum in connection with their Environmental Studies 'Houses and Homes' project, while the seniors visited farms at Littery, Gairnieston and Kinnermit.

The children's drama lessons led to performances to parents and other groups in Turriff. *Jack and the Beanstalk* (1985), *Snow-White and the Seven Dwarfs* (1986) and *Cinderella* (1988) were highlights.

Area school councils set up in 1975 were replaced by individual School Boards in 1989. Fintry's board had seven members - four parents, one teacher and two co-opted members. The aim was to forge closer links between teachers, parents, the wider community and the education authorities.

Cinderella, 6 December 1988: Back: Elizabeth Roberts, Alexandra Anderson, John Ledingham, Callum Pirie, Colin Pirie, David McKay, John McKay, David Rennie, Lorna Rendall, Louise Benzie, Adele Ledingham, Cameron Anderson (behind Adele). **Middle:** Kevin McLeod, Andrew Norrie, Louise Papiez, Gillian Norrie, Duncan Gray, Shelley Sim. **Front:** Gordon Sharp, Mark Green, Allan Sharp, Colin Mackie, Stephen Anderson, Martin Reid, Gordon Cowie, Brian Masson, Claire Cassie.

Technology

Fintry's first computer was bought in 1984 from school funds and by the early 1990s the pupils were learning to use Apple Mac and BBC. An Easter Fayre raised money to buy a BBC computer. A group of parents spent time classifying and cataloguing in 1992 when a library area for the pupils was set up.

Special occasions

The school visited Haddo House and met Prince Charles in 1977, the Queen's Silver Jubilee year. A Farm Open Day at Slackadale in 1983 raised money for good causes and school funds. Senior pupils sailed on the new lake at Slackadale, there was a football tournament, and the school took part in a mini Highland Games for Turriff Round Table Gala in 1989.

That year the new school celebrated its 25th anniversary, with research and visits from former pupils. Pupils planted trees at Wrae for National Tree Planting Week in November 1992, and they enjoyed their first Disco in 1994. Sports Day was now based on athletics skills, and the children competed in the Fintry Challenge.

The 5-14 Programme which was introduced in the 1990s was an attempt to define the contents and objectives of the curriculum, and satisfy the need for assessment, after the freedom of the Primary Memorandum. Scottish teachers adapted national testing to suit their situation, but the guiding principles of 'balance, breadth and continuity' provided a new emphasis on oral and problem-solving skills, a 'more consistent, continuous learning experience', and continuity on transfer to secondary school.

Memories 1965-2003

The community view

George Norrie: Generally, everybody was impressed with the new building. We had great difficulty persuading [the council] we didn't need a huge playing field for a small school. They did compromise and decide to acquire a little bit less than the original plan.

With this brand new building with the community hall, it was such an improvement, we were quite happy. There were no tears when we saw the old buildings being demolished.

It was the hub of the community, the school, and a new headmaster or headmistress, we made a point of making ourselves known.

The day that the new school was opened, we had a big dance in the new school hall that night. It was well attended and very good. I would say maybe 150; the new hall was full.

[School numbers were] down to at one point in the low twenties, and there was quite a lot of thought about the likelihood of it being closed. The people in the district didna want that to happen, and it was always nice if a new family came in, and that'll be another three that'll be at Fintry School.

Three former pupils

Alfie Cheyne (1969-76): I went on the bus to start wi. An old Zander's Bluebird bus, with a half-cab for the driver, and a conductress as well. We was taen doon and dropped at Findale, and then walked from Findale up to Fintry School.

I definitely cycled from the age of six on, at least a whole year before my brother started, and then the two o us cycled together. The bike was too big for me, so my father made a little flat wooden seat and we wrapped it up wi cloots and stuff, so when I was sitting on it, my feet could reach the pedals.

You had your black gymmies, and that's what you wore at school. Your shoes went in to the little cages and you hung your jackets up. And everybody had proper leather schoolbags.

In Primary 1, one lunchtime, Harry and I were playing, but we ran into a lassie wi this trolley o sand,

and she started howling and crying. No inquiry, nothing whatsoever, the two of us just promptly marched straight into Mr Findlay's office, and belted. And here was me, five years old, and how many months… he only belted me once, Harry got three, he's a couple o years older than me, he was seven,… [we were] mesmerised, what we had done wrong.

The school car used to deliver the meals at Fintry. They cooked them at Crudie. There was nobody that didna take school meals. The milk was another thing, you got your bottlie o milk in a morning, a sma glass bottle o milk every day. But that stopped. There was nobody in the year under us, and then just my brother was the only intake in the next year, and because we'd grown older, he was the only one that got free milk. There was a big bit in the Press, the milkman had to come to Fintry with one bottle o milk.

We had a visiting music teacher, and he was a vindictive nasty man, well, he did it to anybody who spoke, [he] came over, and lifted you off the seat, by pulling your lug. He twisted your lug as hard as he possibly could, and he used to lift you right up, pulling, pulling, pulling, but whilst he was doing it, he took great pleasure, he used to stick his tongue out at the side o his mouth, and bite his tongue, as he was doing it, a nasty man, is all I can possibly ever describe him as.

It would hae been total Doric, there was nae anything else. We were never ever forced to speak anything else. I've lost a bit o my tongue, because I've worked a lot overseas, and I'm dealing wi people on an international basis. And I dinna speak the Doric like I should dae. The teachers, they would hae spoken properly.

We didn't do Robbie Burns, put it that way, or maybe one poem about Rabbie Burns time, and that would have been it. I did *Geordie Wabster,* the Doric poem, at a school concert, recited that off by heart.

There was a blackboard right along the wall, and if you grated your nails on it, abody skirled. Anne Sinclair, aye, she was a nice person. You know, if a teacher belts you and anither ane comes, at that age, you're gaun to be completely thingmied wi the teachers, so… I think she was a good teacher.

Mrs Tawse was very, very good at visits. We went to Tain, I remember, that was Primary 6 or 7, the last year, we went away to Tain on a school trip, we stayed away for a few days. Some friend o hers, had this big house, the station master's house, and we went away up in Robertson o Cuminestown's bus, and we did all sorts o stuff up there.

I remember we were at a cheese factory, I think we did a distillery, a number o things… she definitely had a different mind-set from just classroom teaching. She had a broader vision, gave you a greater curriculum if you like.

We had a huge map o the world, and this huge bit, the United Soviet Socialist Republic I remember it had on it, this massive bit o Russia, and of course, Russia was feared at that time because it was bred intae us that this was the enemy. This was the Cold War period, of course. We were always on edge about the Russians.

It must have been '72, '73, we tracked a climb up Everest. That was up on the wall, a big map of Mount Everest, every day we tracked where these climbers were.

The school magazine was done on a duplicating machine, and this blue ink, and they cranked the handle. And there was a TV, that's right, and we aa used to ging doon into the hall to watch programmes on TV at a certain time.

And then once a week Tommy Wark the minister came as well. We sang hymns and that, and he telt the Bible stories, and I was always amazed because a man used to drive him in a taxi, and used to sit in a car or a taxi all the time he was there, waiting for him, and I used to think, what a lot o money that must be costing.

North Sea oil, that was hardly spoken about, yet it was going, up and going, just, yes, but then it was '76 ere I left Fintry, and it was booming then. We covered a lot of the traditional industries, the linoleum in Kirkcaldy, and the flax and the jute in Dundee, and all that stuff. We were taught all about crop rotation, and the feudal system. And a bit about our fishing, and agriculture, a bit about coal-mining, as well, I think every term there was a wee project in different things, but oil really didna come into it that much.

We did the Lowlands, looked at the different produce in the different areas. And we covered a bit about the British Isles; we had to learn every county in the British Isles, yes. Learn by heart every one, where they were, what the name was, and we had the capital, the main town in each area. I enjoyed all that sort of stuff.

There was some fascinating stuff as well, in the big class cupboard. Some teacher must hae been abroad, there was coral, there was a lot o stuff like that, some stuff oot o the sea, stuff you'd never have seen or heard of, come fae different parts …

Looking out the window in the big class, we used to stare oot the window at these great swoops o starlings, thousands o starlings, between the school and Slackadale. The whole sky used to be black, pure black wi starlings, great flocks. I remember once we saw a stoat, in its winter coat, all white, through the Fintry classroom window, in the gardens.

I suppose it was a bit strange for a school to be in the country, like that, we didna have a school garden. Now King Edward had a school garden, and the boys there used to grow stuff, but we didna at Fintry.

It was WRI that organised the Halloween party, it wasna the school, and aa the school kids, aa came to the Rural party. I do remember Santa came, cause I remember Murray Ledingham looking out through the curtains, saying, that's Santy coming doon by Fintry Smiddy… and we're aa sitting there waiting, it's silly the things you remember.

Why we'd go to Peterhead on a picnic, one o the coldest places on earth! I remember when the bus dropped us off, my mother and me walked for what seemed like miles to get a saddlebag for my bike, from Robertson's bicycle shop in Peterhead, not far from the Kirkburn Mills, so that was the big event o that picnic.

I think we had more of a sports day at the school, because what used to happen was aa the local farmers used to come, John Ledingham, George Norrie, Sandy Benzie, and aa these guys used to come wi pockets full o cash, it was pennies, five pence and maybe a ten pence

Fintry football team, 1974: Back: David Mutch, Gary Thomson, Richard Stafford, Gordon Henry, Alfred Cheyne.
Front: Keith Mitchell, Kenneth Cheyne.

if you were really lucky for running a race.

Some chappie here now, him and his friend, used to go into the classroom, the upstairs classroom, at lunchtime and make me run roon and roon and roon the fitba pitch at lunchtime, and if I stopped they came oot wi whin bushes and jabbed me with them to keep me running - horrible experience. I mean, there was some fun days and aa, a lot o nice kids, so there was good times as well.

It was a big playground, it was a good playground. We'd bike sheds doon at the bottom, we used to play hide and seek a lot, there was a shrubbery, poor shrubbery wi us going through it aa the time.

There was the Bogstrups, there was Christina and Esther, their mother was German. There was a lot o families, it was aa families, there was whole families there. I suppose everybody looked after each other, at the end o the day.

I joined the Scouts in Turriff, and I was seeing a bigger world, and then you were still going doon the road to that little schoolie at Fintry, and you were looking for bigger things in life by that stage. I think a lot o these rural country schools are great in the early years o developing, but as you're getting up into Primary 5, 6, 7, you're really ready for a change, because you're only in a little peer group o half a dozen folk.

Richard Stafford (1973-76): We got to Backhill of Plaidy towards the end of the summer of 1973, and when my sister and I started at Fintry I think we brought the numbers up to fifteen. That picture, the 1974 football team, they were all the boys big enough to play football.

I do remember the first night, having had the first day at school, being at home when all of a sudden there was a knock on the door and Gary Thomson and... I've forgotten the other lad's name... Gordon, had turned up. I think it was harvest time, they'd got a lift across on a combine or a grain trailer most of the way. They'd come across to see the new lad and see where he lived and so to have a play out before going back on another grain trailer just as it was getting dark - mates from day one.

There was a school car, Mr Kendrick drove that, a big Vauxhall Victor or something, and did several runs to get all the children to school who weren't close enough to walk. In the summer I used to cycle, because it was only a couple or three miles from Plaidy across to Fintry. It was quite pleasant in the summer. Getting home, the small kids went first and the older ones had to wait.

Mrs. Sinclair was a very friendly teacher. Mrs. Tawse was a lot stricter. I remember one day she apologised to me, because she'd asked the previous day what a fathom was, and I said it was six feet. She thought it was something different, and she said I was wrong, and I knew I was right. Obviously I'd made her question herself, cause she'd gone home and checked it out, and came in the next day and apologised.

I've an abiding love of Iceland and I go there whenever I can. It was Mrs. Sinclair started it by reading us Icelandic sagas. We used to finish the days with some stories, and she was into Icelandic sagas at one stage.

I certainly remember doing woodwork up on the stage. There was quite a good supply of tools and wood and things. I made a forklift truck out of balsa wood. I do remember making a clay Loch Ness Monster which I've still got somewhere, so there obviously was an art or handicraft class in the upstairs classroom.

Sometimes, the local words were asked to be replaced with proper ones, purely for grammatical English. You can't write *'fit'* for *'what'* when writing something, so I think the local kids were encouraged, were told to write English as it should be written. I know a couple of kids sometimes struggled to always remember to put the proper word in.

As far as speaking, everybody spoke the same dialect, it wasn't really identified as being a dialect, it was just how people spoke. Richard and Penny spoke slightly different because they'd come from Somerset, and there was another lad, Keith Mitchell, who was from England.

I went off to Glengonar, that was the year before I went up to the academy, a school camp in the Peebles direction. It was a chance to meet other kids that had come from similar rural schools so that we at least knew a few faces when we went to the Academy. There were people from Cuminestown and places like that.

It must have been summertime, we did outdoor things. There was a big hill nearby on the other side of the river, so we were out reasonably late in the evenings doing stuff. We went off to Edinburgh Zoo and places like that, and Glasgow's Transport Museum.

We twinned with a small school on Skye. It was Digg School, right up on the north-east coast of Skye, we had been writing letters to the kids of Digg School and we were paired off with people of our own age, the boys with boys and the girls with girls. The chap I was with, he lived on a small croft, and I stayed and had a couple of meals.

We slept in the school hall, in sleeping bags on the floor, with Mrs. Tawse and the bus driver. Poor old bus driver didn't get anything better than a sleeping bag on the floor as well. From Fintry across to Skye was a bit of a hike in itself, a day each way. I know we stopped off for a cup of coffee at Mrs. Tawse's parents on the way back.

I spent a fair bit of time helping on the croft, investigating the area, and a couple of trips out from there. It was certainly something out of the ordinary, and we spent a lot of time in the classroom comparing the sort of farming that was done on Skye, the crofting there, with the sort of farming that was done in our area.

There were no big farms, like Slackadale, or anything like that, doing pigs or great acres of potatoes. The crofting over on Skye is just purely sheep, and a few beef cattle probably. They were busy cutting peat, and doing all the bits and pieces, and also being quite close, right on the sea, there was small-scale fishing.

We went to a big park in Aberdeen or somewhere like that, and had lots of running around and playing children's games, running about the park getting tired and hungry and thirsty. A gaggle of mums would come and assist the teachers, making sure nobody got lost or overly hurt or unfed.

We used to go swimming at Turriff pool. The coach would pick us up, then the King Edward kids and go into Turriff. On sports day King Edward came across to us, we had a bigger playing field, behind the school.

The boys had great fun climbing all over the roof. You climb up the gutter, as you look at the building there's the hall on your right, a down pipe on the corner of the building there, and if you climbed that you get onto the roof of that bit, and from there on to the main hall roof. The trick was to race each other up on to the ridge of the roof before the teachers caught you.

If it was dry we'd play football on the field at the back. From memory, there were bicycle sheds as you look down the playground on the left. There was a septic tank, and the cover disappeared or got broken. Someone put their foot in one day and got covered in gunk, but we shouldn't have been round the back anyway.

Louise Grieve (1984-91, and current parent): We used to get a little car to Fintry School. Willie Wilson, he was such a nice man. There was just a few of us, it's a minibus now. And I have got to pay for my kids, although they're zoned for Fintry School. We've got to pay for the bus, but years ago, Mum and Dad never. I enjoyed going in the little car.

I hated the milk, it used to be curdled at the top, and the birds used to peck in it. It was Mrs McHattie that was my teacher, I loved her; she was a really good teacher.

Everything, I would say, I loved at Fintry School. Art, sometimes we got art teachers, sometimes we didna. If we didna, for that term, Mrs McHattie or Mrs Findlay, there was always somebody that did something wi you. Mrs Hay used to come out, and do sewing classes. We made cushions; it was just putting your hand to it.

Every term we had a project, and if there was something that coincided wi your project, you would be daein stories. Down in Mrs McHattie's class you always got a story. It was either before dinner time or before we went home in the afternoon; that was just a calm down, a five-minute time before you go, just to say goodbye, and see you in the morning.

Because I was the only girl in the class, and as I grew older, I tended to go in at break times, dinner time maybe, and ask if they were wanting help to dae onything. There was a helper, Jill Collie, at that time, and we used to bind books, staple things thegither, do leaflets, just little odd jobs.

But the classroom hasnae changed, apart fae your whiteboards. It used to be blackboards, and just aa technology now. Very rarely did we get to use a computer, and I think the majority has computers. You've got your Glow and whatever now.

I think there were maybe two computers at the most, it just seemed to be they had to work fa was getting on. If you had a project, you'd write oot your things, or you'd print oot if it was to go up on the wall, that was just because they were wanting a good copy.

That was your last day thing or last couple o days, you'd wipe doon aa the books and the shelves and that.

Some things, like the Halloween parties, we used to go in to big style, everyone was dressed up, and party games, it was a big thing, Hallowe'en, your neep lantern, abody put a lot o effort into it. Same wi the Christmas parties, they're good, Fintry School's always haen good Christmas parties, but we had it old-fashioned, Mrs McHattie played the piano, now it's just aa doon to tapes, and CDs.

We occasionally had Christmas concerts, the majority we had pantomimes. Anne Rendall, she was awfy good in daein the costumes for the pantomimes. Aa the mums used to come and help at the busy times, practising for the pantomimes.

Primary 6, 7, when it was your last year, you got to hae a big part in it. There was Cinderella, Snow White, and we used to hae two sittings as well, afternoon used to be oot the door, and I always remember when you had a part or sung yersel, there was a clock at the end o the hall, and I think it's maybe still there, and we were always told, to look at that clock and dinna look doon, and sing your heart out.

The *Grand Old Duke of York*... what's that ane you clap in, you clap oot, I canna even mind the names. I could do them; they were good old traditional dances.

The Gay Gordons, or *Dashing White Sergeant.*

Before the summertime, we was always ootside, and practising for sports days. Again that was another big event. Sports days was really like a mini-competition atween aa the kids. I remember I won the trophies quite a few times, there was always me and Andrew Norrie, we were good at doing high jump, and tension was on to see fa would actually get the highest score.

Your inter-school sports, you used to go with aa the little schools roon aboot, Crudie, Fisherford. You used to take your picnic. It used to be one year at Fintry, one year at King Edward, one year at Crudie, but nowadays it just seems to be at Crudie, whether it's a bigger pitch, cause there's quite a lot o pupils when aa the schools are thegither now; the littler schools used to be 30, 40, and that was it, but some o the little schools can actually be about 60, 70 noo.

Quite often we went to Gairnieston pond, walking there, we went to Slackadale lake, it could just be a walk to hae a look, if you were daein a project, look for tadpoles, just nature things. I remember doing something doon at Slackadale lake, maybe that was through Fintry School, canoeing and aa different activities. That was a good day.

We went to different farms, like a dairy farm. That's faur it's aa changed now, health and safety disna let you dae that. There was quite often people came in, wi lambs or chickens, just to show you.

We did hae Scottish days, like your St Andrew's Day, we maybe dressed up, or put on something Scottish, maybe tartan, I think they celebrate St Andrew's Day more now than what we did when I was at school.

No, we was always writing English words, it was nae Doric or naething. Amongst ourselves, I think, yes, we did speak it. It's just what you've been brought up with at home, but when you were speaking to a teacher, you tend to put on your English voice, and the same wi them, when they were speaking to you. But there was occasionally your teacher maybe did say, *'Och, come here'*. It was just so relaxed, if you did speak Doric to them they wouldna gie you a row for it.

There was the bike sheds, and we went doon there, if

it was raining, and sometimes we would crawl up the walls, which we shouldna have done. The swings and the seesaw were always the favourite. We didna hae a rota, it just seemed to be first come, first served, but you did get a shot eventually. The seesaw was quite lethal sometimes if you got a boy on the other end, they would try and flick you up.

'Kiss, cuddle and torture' was another ane. The majority was boys at school that times, they aye seemed to choose the kiss… and it seemed to get quite boring efter a whilie. You catch them, you say *'kiss, cuddle or torture'*, and they've got to choose. If they say *'kiss'*, you've got to peck them on the cheek, if they say *'torture'*, you kind of pushed them with your knee in their bum, and *'cuddle'* is cuddle.

We played hopscotch, used to hae numbers and draw chalk on the ootside, that was good; skipping games where you used to join heaps of skipping ropes thegither, so sometimes there was the whole school, one would jump in, and you'd hae a song wi it, I really canna mind fit it went like, and sometimes you would jump oot again, or one would jump in and dae a few skips and then another ane would jump in, until you were all in, then you would jump oot individually. Sometimes we'd just hae a bit o paper and pen and doodle ootside.

My sister was getting bullied by one of the Turriff boys until one day she stood up for herself, it was just little things like pushing down the brae at the back o the school, and he would push her and push her, push her so far, and she turned round one day and I dinna ken if she'd nipped him or what. I think Mum and the boy's mum was taen in to school and… it wasn't until then that his mum realised that he was actually bullying. Efter that, it was sorted, but there wasna a lot o that there.

There was another incomer, that's horrible saying incomer, Mark Curtis, he was German. He was really difficult to understand for a start, but he really came on wi his English and he was telling us how to say it in German and then we were trying to tell him what to say. They settled in fine as well.

School photo, June 1981: Back: Alexandra Harpin, Andrew Benzie, Adam Gray, Colin Allan, Mark Andrew, Shona Hepburn, and 2 others unknown. **Middle:** Neil Benzie, Michael Rennie, Angela Ledingham, Linda Hepburn, Gary Andrew, Stephanie Allan, John Riach, Kevin Gray, Andrew Riach, Jamie Tarbet. **Front:** Keith Rendall, Steven Lansen, Lynsey Benzie, Mark Allan, Toni-Jane Harpin, Richard Anderson, James Gaul, Morna Matthews, Angus Pirie, Christine Benzie. Mrs Sheila McHattie and Mrs Catriona Tawse.

Four former teachers

Catriona Tawse (head teacher 1974-82): We had educational outings to local places including a distillery where in these less rule-bound days all of us were given a miniature sample (to take home to parents, of course).

Children were responsive and well-behaved. Happy to say some went on to greater things.

Sheila McHattie (infant teacher 1974-2003): I went to Fintry in 1974. My daughter was only two years and a month, and she was allowed to come to school with me. They were so scarce of teachers. At that time I only had eleven pupils, so she just sat and amused herself and at intervals and lunch times she was away with the rest, playing games. When the Primary 1s used to sit down to do their reading, she used to take a chair as well, and sit with them. The parents were really nice to her as well; they looked upon her as another wee pupil. I think there was only twenty-one in the whole school, you were just like a mum to them.

I usually took them altogether for a story just to start off the day, then I gave them their individual activities, because it was more or less individual teaching when you had only 11.

We always did RE, once a week, and before they went home, we used to sing a hymn all together. At the end of term there'd be a service and the mums were invited as well, and the dads and the grannies, whoever. It was like a social occasion. There was a cup of tea at the end of it, and a chat.

There was this Ruth and Andy Lovell, they're from Peterhead Mission. They come round maybe once a month or six weeks. They certainly brought RE alive to the pupils, got them all involved. He was a really good singer, and he'd the guitar. They sang some good-going songs for the kids. Then he had pictures, and little figures to stick on to them, and he got the children out to stick them on.

He never stood still, he was moving about the whole time. He really brought the stories alive. Then he'd a puppet that he took out at the end, and he'd ask Freddie the puppet what he'd thought of the story. Freddie was always dressed either in his football strip or

Cowboys and Indians, May 1975: Gary Andrew, Fraser Mitchell, Jonathan Kendrick, Andrew Benzie, Lesley Thomson, Carol Jamieson, Gillian McHattie, Alison Mitchell, Colin Allan. **(Standing at back)** Stephen Bowie, Penny Stafford, Derek Andrew.

his rugby strip. The kids looked forward to him coning.

There was a sewing and home economics teacher, Hazel Milne. It was just fine a new face coming in to the school. Especially the girls, they just loved her. Whiles she did crocheting and knitting, whiles she did cookery. I think she did knitting with the boys as well, and sewing. It was fine getting different ideas from a visiting teacher as well. We were pretty lucky at the beginning, and then as the cuts started, we didna get so many visiting teachers.

Sometimes we had meetings with one of the advisers, all the Primary 1, 2, teachers. She was speaking about what you were actually doing in the classroom with the kids, and she gave you good ideas for work cards and things like that.

The Ginn reading scheme, it was good. Some of the books were a bit repetitive, but it got them reading. Then they took out the Oxford reading scheme, and it had good stories, but a few fell by the wayside. It just didna seem to give them the basics, as the Ginn did. Then we did the phonics alongside it as well. Well, there's *'jolly phonics'*, they've to learn two three sounds a week, which is fine for the ones that are good, but the ones that are finding it harder, I really dinna know how they get on. Certainly the actions are good, it's a fun thing for them, but I just think two or three sounds are quite a lot a week. I wasna working with them long enough to know what advantage they were. It was supposed to get them writing stories and that quicker.

We often did weather, and the seasons, we did Holland, and Switzerland and Australia, we did the Vikings, the Romans, and castles, just castles in general, and nursery rhymes and fairy tales. Space - that was a favourite.

Towards the end of my teaching you had to get them to fit into a category with the 5-14, but you usually managed to work round it and get it to fit in. It was more the planning that was hard, all the different bits to fit in the curriculum, I dinna know why Aberdeenshire council didna just come out with a scheme, because everybody was wondering what were the best projects to fit into the different categories. They never did, but at

'We are the Champions', June 1980: Front: Andrew Benzie, Angela Ledingham, Jonathan Kendrick, Alison Mitchell, Fraser Mitchell, Stephanie Allan, Kevin Gray. (**Back:** unnamed).

the little cluster meetings we used to swap ideas.

The kids fairly liked their projects. It would be a three year rota, because you had the children for three year. When you did farming, that went down well at Fintry. You had super drawings and pictures fae aa the boys. There was a lot of competition about who started combining first, particularly with the boys.

If we were doing fairy tales or nursery rhymes, we might have gone into Storybook Glen, and if it was fishing, we went to Fraserburgh, sometimes the fish market in Macduff. If it was the seashore, it was Banff beach, looking at the rocks there.

One really good one was travel; we took the bus from Fintry to Inverurie, we went on the train at Inverurie, and went to Aberdeen, and got the bus in Aberdeen that took us out to Dyce airport, and that time we actually got across the tarmac and into a plane. The kids just thought that was wonderful, because some of them had never been on an aeroplane. They couldna believe it when the pilot came and spoke to them. And then the bus met us again at the airport and took us

▶ **Letter from the Queen**, 1987

BUCKINGHAM PALACE

11th March 1987

To: The Pupils of P1-3,
Fintry School,
Turriff,
Aberdeenshire

I write to thank you for all the pictures which you sent to Buckingham Palace for The Queen to see.

Her Majesty thought it was kind of you to draw these for her, and I am to tell you The Queen was interested to hear about your project.

Susan Hussey

Lady-in-Waiting

back to Fintry. That was a really good one, it just all flowed. They spoke about it for weeks after.

We'd really good parents, supportive parents, and you'd no problem getting parents to come and help you. Most of the homes had two parents as well. Even ex-parents helped. Old John Ledingham from Fintry Farm, he'd send down a box of tangerines for the Christmas party.

George Norrie, he built the lake at Slackadale, if there was something interesting, he'd just phone down to the school and say, what about taking the children round the lake the day and I'll meet you. If there was a sow pigged, and she'd quite a lot of litter, he'd say what about coming up and see the piglets this morning, and you just went. He was so good.

We were lucky, with the Benzies as well, they had a lake, and Mabel would phone up, some fine days, would

▶ **'Poor Molly'(death of a pet), 31 March 1989:** **Back:** Sharp twin, Duncan Gray, Sharp twin. **Front:** Alexandra Anderson, Adele Ledingham, Shelley Sim, Colin Mackie.

you like to take the children up and have a look in the pond, and once you'd looked, Mabel would have juice and all the nice pieces for the kids, it was like a mini picnic.

Same with Jean Norrie at the chalet at the lake. They were really lucky kids going to Fintry. They were quite proud of their school, the children enjoy it as well.

Your requisition wasna just that much at that time, by the time you got books and pencils and textbooks, you were glad of some extra money for some bigger equipment. Of course we had to pay for buses when we did go our outings.

Sometimes if we did the Teddy Bears' Picnic at Haddo House, we'd have a Ranger there, took them round the trees, talked about the creatures in the woods. I remember doing Night Time for a project once, about October, November time. So we went in the bus to Haddo House, some mums as well, it would have been about half past three, quarter to four when we arrived, it was just beginning to get dark, and the children were skipping about. And then we were back to the bus about six, it was pitch dark, they were holding on to our hands. It was so funny, they werena going away in front.

When I newly went to Fintry, I'd to test them for spelling, about Primary 2, to see if they needed Learning Support or additional help, then we had the national testing at levels, before I left.

A lot of it was a waste of time, because you didna test them until you were pretty sure they would pass, it was just a bit of proof for parents. But they began to get it earlier and earlier, and some bright little kids did manage it, especially the maths; the language was a wee bit harder. It was just the time it took. You still had your class, and you had to find time to do the testing and hope that the others got on with their work and didna need any help.

We must have been doing the school as a project. It was Mrs Findlay's time, and her husband was head teacher at Markethill, so it made [an exchange day] a bit easier. The Fintry ones were a bit lost, I would hae said; at break time they just stayed near the door. The area we were in there was about 30 - the noise! I think they

Nativity, December 1979: Angel: Morna Matthews. Shepherds: Richard Anderson, Stephanie Allan, Angela Ledingham, Neil Benzie. Mary: Susan Anderson. Joseph: Andrew Riach. Kings: Mark Allan, James Gaul.

were a wee bit scared, just over-awed by it all.

What I didna like very much was drama. It's always a bit scarce especially at the start, when you'd only 11 children, a lot of them doing things. You didna have an audience.

There was a sponsored walk round by Yonderton and Gairnieston one Sunday morning and they had soup and sandwiches in the school hall afterwards. That was well turned out. A lot of dads came as well.

You got aa this money to spend. Usually we're wanting to make money. There was the projector screen, we got staplers, laminators and things like that. The money would have been better put in to books and things like that. You weren't allowed to buy books. We were lucky, one of the mums, her husband worked in an oil company, and he had a whip round and we had a whole new reading scheme from that company

Helen Findlay (head teacher 1982-93): The people were all so friendly. I was not teaching when we came to Fintry, but one morning the assistant didn't turn up and I got a call and went up and that was me until 1993.

I remember James [Michie], the director, coming through, and saying it was a beautiful new school, you'll be pleased to be here, and I said, yes, it's very nice, but.. 'Come on then, out with the "buts"'. 'I can't understand why all the blackboards for the children are all up there, when they should be down here where they can reach.'

'Oh yes, we'll get that sorted', so sure enough, he did.

I always found the children got on well together, I think it was because they needed each other. They had to get on because they had only enough to make a football team, so there wasn't a lot of aggro.

There used to be outings, like maybe the Cooper Park in Elgin, or Tarlair, maybe the Winter Gardens, then that kind of annual picnic went out of favour. If you were going out of the school, it had to be part of whatever you were doing in the classroom. It was usually locally, maybe to a farm. The children enjoyed

School Photo, June 1989: Mrs McHattie and Mrs Helen Findlay. **Back:** Martin Morrison, Colin Mackie, Brian Masson, Andrew Norrie, Duncan Gray, Mark Green, Martin Reid, Gordon Cowie, Steven Anderson. **Middle:** Claire Cassie, Clare McLeod, Adele Ledingham, John McKay, Alan Sharp, Alexandra Anderson, Gordon Sharp, Kevin McLeod, Shelley Sim, Louise Papiez. **Front:** Louise Benzie, John Ledingham, Lorna Rendall, David McKay, David Rennie, Colin Pirie, Cameron Anderson, Callum Pirie, Gillian Norrie.

that, then the sports, we grew that we would have a Sports Day against Crudie, then all the small schools joined in.

We had the old-fashioned [computers], then a more modern one, one in the office, one in the infant room, and one upstairs. The children used it and some of them were better than I [was] at using it. If anything went wrong, Duncan Gray usually managed to sort it out.

Just once, when we were in the schoolhouse, we had one boy overnight. A storm blew up very quickly, and the parents couldn't get in. But the grieve from Slackadale came down with the Land Rover, he took a lot of them home, so we were just left with one, and that was the boy Dalgarno from Badentyre.

It grew that the schools were closed quickly, remember there was a girlie died at Inverurie, walking home, and after that you got a warning. I had an arrangement with some of the outlying parents that if they thought their road was closing, they phoned and I'd arrange for the bus to come.

Some of them did exceptionally well, others you

Paradise Woods, May 1988: Left to right – Mark Green, Allan Sharp, Brian Masson, Shellie Sim.

CLAAS
5610

think could have done better. That's just testing, isn't it? The thing I did mind was when they said you couldn't do tables and mental arithmetic. I still did it but I wasn't supposed to. You weren't allowed to do spelling as such, and you weren't supposed to take note of the spelling when you were correcting their work but I couldn't put up with that. You couldn't do the alphabet and sounding out the words, [now] they're all back to doing that.

There was a mixed message [on Doric]; it was a case of finding your own level, and so we tried to do poetry, and do the Burns competition. Actually some of the English children who came in were quite good at doing the Doric.

[Pantomimes] were a lot of hard work. The parents made all the costumes and so on. It was great fun, but the restrictions got, you couldn't take photographs, and you couldn't take a video, so you felt is it really worth it?

It was a shame, for you often found the best children on the stage were not necessarily the best in the classroom and it gave them a chance to shine. They were

WINDSOR CASTLE

To:

The Pupils in Classes 1-3,
c/o Miss S.M.c Hattie,
Fintry School,
Turriff,
Aberdeenshire.

I am commanded by The Queen to thank you all for your letter.

Although it was not possible for Her Majesty to attend your school concert, The Queen thought it was very kind of you to invite her and Her Majesty hopes that you all enjoyed it.

I am enclosing some leaflets which you may like to have and thank you all once again for your letter.

Henriette Abel Smith

Lady-in-Waiting

3rd April, 1991.

Slackadale 1999

Craigston Castle, January 2003: Left to right: Lauren Capstick, Logan Smith, Charley Stephen, Colin Thompson, Mark Morrison.

always dying to have a part; when I said, the three ugly sisters are really meant to be boys, dressed up, that was alright, they would dress up.

We used to take [the pre-school children] in one morning a week, for maybe six weeks before they came. We had a meeting first with the parents to tell them what it was all about, and then we took the children in and gave some of the ones from the lower classroom a chance to be up with the older ones as well.

Jan Filshie (Head Teacher 1993-2000): One of my strongest memories was how important the school was

Mrs McHattie's retiral, 4 July 2003: Left to right – Grant Reidford, Andrew Hepburn, Matthew Capstick, with Savannah Gray in front.

in the life of the community and vice versa. Parents were very supportive and they worked tirelessly to fund raise and offer any help they could. There was a great feeling of teamwork within the school and the pupils were a pleasure to teach.

I remember many successful events that involved pupils, parents and the community:

- A sponsored walk with all ages taking part and a warming plate of soup at the end
- Always a full house for all our concerts
- Planting our time capsule in the small patch of garden in 2000
- Inter-school football tournaments and sports days
- Tray bakes, coffee mornings and always a fantastic spread
- Trying to develop a garden area on the bank at the back of the school
- Working closely with other schools in our group
- School residential trips, in particular to Carbisdale Castle and Youth Hostel in Glasgow following the story of *'The Desperate Journey'*.

Fintry today

▶ School Catchment Area 2011 (COURTESY OF ABERDEENSHIRE COUNCIL)

The establishment of the devolved Scottish Executive in 1999 led to the introduction of the Curriculum for Excellence, covering ages 3 to 18. Its aim was to return some freedom of choice of curriculum to the teachers, within four 'capacities' of 'successful learners, confident individuals, responsible citizens and effective contributors'. Mutual respect and trust are of prime importance throughout the school community.

Literacy, numeracy, health and well-being are the core elements of the curriculum, with the aim of enabling progression and personal achievement for every learner, of whatever age or ability. There is emphasis on Scottish history and language, and on respecting the local culture of the children. It is also important that learning is enjoyable for all learners.

The North Lanarkshire Active Literacy scheme is in use throughout Aberdeenshire, with new reading, writing and spelling approaches. Outdoor learning and Eco-school activities promote healthy living and environmental awareness. Aberdeenshire's Active Schools initiative provides blocks of sports tuition through the year, and the Turriff feeder schools have an annual inter-school sports day.

Her Majesty's Inspectorate of Education (HMIe) carried out a full inspection at Fintry in June 2011, and evaluated the school as good in improving its performance, in providing learners' experiences and in meeting learning needs. Judged satisfactory were the delivery of the curriculum and improvement through self-evaluation.

The report noted as the particular strengths of the school: the quality and care of relationships between staff and children, the contribution of parents, the local community and visitors that enhance children's learning experience, support for children experiencing difficulties in their learning, the commitment and teamwork of the head teacher and staff to making improvements for learners.

For the school's 180th anniversary in September 2011, pupils studied its history and gathered information, written and oral, from parents, grandparents and community members. The celebratory Open Day was attended by over 100 former pupils, including a few of nearly ninety years of age. The adventure trail, funded by parents and the National Lottery, was officially opened, and former and current pupils shared their experiences of learning and play in a well-loved community school.

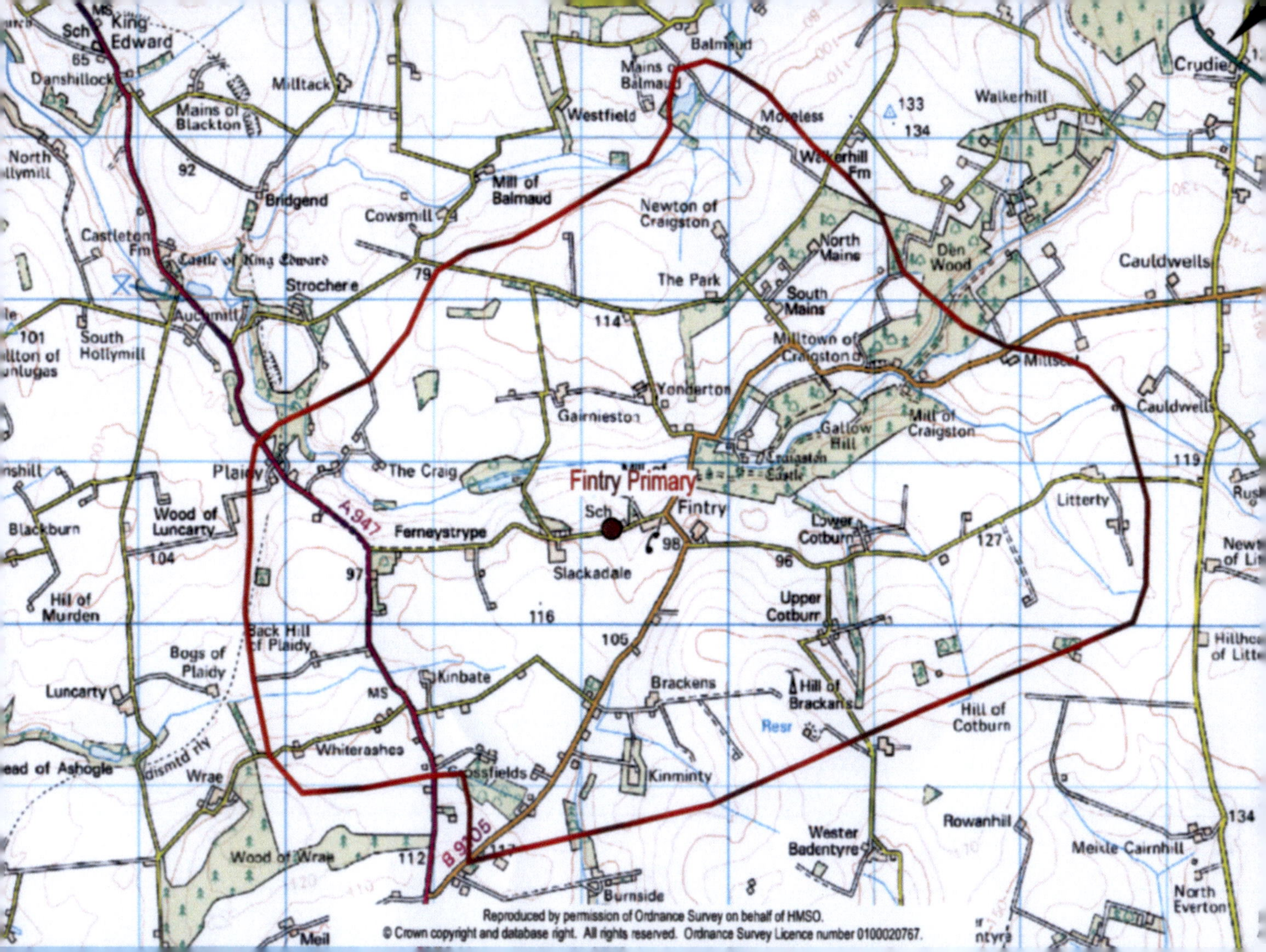
Fintry Primary
Sch
King Edward
Danshillock
Milltack
Mains of Blackton
Balmaud
Mains of Balmaud
Westfield
Moreless
Crudie
Walkerhill
Walkerhill Fm
North Hollymill
Bridgend
Mill of Balmaud
Cowsmill
Newton of Craigston
Castleton Fm
Castle of King Edward
Strochere
North Mains
Den Wood
Cauldwells
The Park
South Mains
Auchmill
South Hollymill
Milltown of Craigston
Millseat
Yonderton
Gairnieston
Mill of Craigston
Gallow Hill
Craigston Castle
Plaidy
The Craig
Fintry
Litterty
Blackburn
Wood of Luncarty
A 947
Ferneystrype
Lower Cotburn
Slackadale
Hill of Murden
Upper Cotburn
Back Hill of Plaidy
Bogs of Plaidy
Kinbate
Luncarty
Brackens
Hill of Brackans
Hill of Cotburn
Resr
Whiterashes
Wrae
Crossfields
Kinminty
Rowanhill
Wester Badentyre
Meikle Cairnhill
Wood of Wrae
B 9105
Burnside
North Everton
Meil
dismtd rly
MS

Head teacher Jane Mack (May 2012)

We're very lucky here, we've got a very supportive staff, and everybody does a little bit extra. It's a nice feeling to come into school every Monday.

If something really interested the children, you could focus on that for two or three days.

The children are much more involved in their own learning. They set targets, they know what their next steps are; they're beginning to evaluate their own work.

We're doing a lot of outdoor learning at the moment, that's the in thing, so they really enjoy that. And we've done a lot more active maths, so we get quite a lot of positive feedback.

There's not that many farming families now, maybe three of four. Quite a lot of trades, like painters, joiners, a lot of lorry drivers, quite a few work in Aberdeen or Inverurie. We've got single parents, a real mixture actually.

The new curriculum is a lot more Scottish. There's a huge emphasis on Scottish history, and Scots language. We

The infant classroom, and Mrs Ogg, May 2011

Senior classroom on Open Day, 2011: Mrs Lorraine Hendry with pupils.

still have a number of native Doric speakers, and I feel they should be encouraged, if that's the language they come to school with, to speak that language.

[The children] still speak about their *'pints'* for their shoelaces, they would never speak about a field, they would always speak about a *'park'*. They would all know what a loon and a quine was, *'fit like'* and things like that.

I've only had one or two who are really keen to write it. Sometimes [incomers] look at the other children blankly when they first get here, but quite often you get a child using Doric words with a very English accent.

They use English where it's appropriate, but some of them might never use English; some of the parents just speak Doric all the time, and have made very successful lives for themselves. I think as long as the children are aware that there are big opportunities out there in the world.

We have to teach Christian religion in the Curriculum for Excellence, one other world religion and obviously personal search, moral sort of things.

We tend to teach the festivals of Christmas and Easter every year, because when we're doing it, we're not telling them that's what they have to believe, we're just saying this is what people who are Christians believe.

We've done all sorts of fancy Christmas plays, but they all end up with the nativity at the end. We've done ones about spacemen, ones about homeless people, and I just thought this year, we're going to go back to basics, because there's something quite sweet about a very old-fashioned nativity play.

A lot of how children behave is how you treat them. If you treat them with respect, I think they're much more likely to behave for you. If you can prevent their behaviour from escalating and you divert them, and if they respect you, they want to behave for you. Most of them want to please you.

We get a huge amount of parental support. Every event we have, we have about 98 percent of the parents turn up. We've got parents in every day this week doing the cycling, parents coming in this afternoon to help sort the books out for the new reading scheme.

They raise money for the school. You just need to say,

Nativity play, 2011

'can you make teas for this event' and they do.

A lot of people say they prefer a smaller school. And certainly I think some pupils do better in a smaller school, although likewise some may do better in a bigger school.

I think in general parents are more supportive than in the big schools. In a small school, if they're not there, they know they're noticed. And I think there's more of a community feel. Everyone feels a part of the school, parents, grandparents, aunties, uncles.

We work an open-door policy, so parents are always welcome, and I think they appreciate that.

You know the pupils, inside out and back to front. You know their mums, their dads, their grannies, their aunties, you know their pets, you know where they live, so if there's a problem at home you know why they're behaving the way they are at school, and you have them from P1 to P7, so you can really treat them as an individual.

There are disadvantages in that if a child doesn't get on with a teacher, they're stuck with them for three or four years.

If a child is in a class where there are only two or three pupils, they maybe don't have a big peer group to mix with, although they do mix with children, younger and older, in a smaller school.

We always go to the pantomime at Christmastime, and we take them to the likes of Techfest in Aberdeen. Two of the boys went to the C'nexx Challenge as they got through.

If we're doing castles, we take them to a castle, if we're doing the seashore, we take them to the seashore, or Macduff Aquarium, just wherever.

When we were looking at the local community, we went on a trip to Turriff and Aberdeen to compare Aberdeen to Turriff and Fintry, a comparison between a village, a town and a city.

And we've been to Satrosphere, to Marischal College Museum, it just depends what your topic is. But we also have a lot of visitors in to school, because it's much cheaper.

We have a lot of theatre groups, we had Zoo Lab. When we were doing the rainforests a chap came in with all these animals from the rainforest.

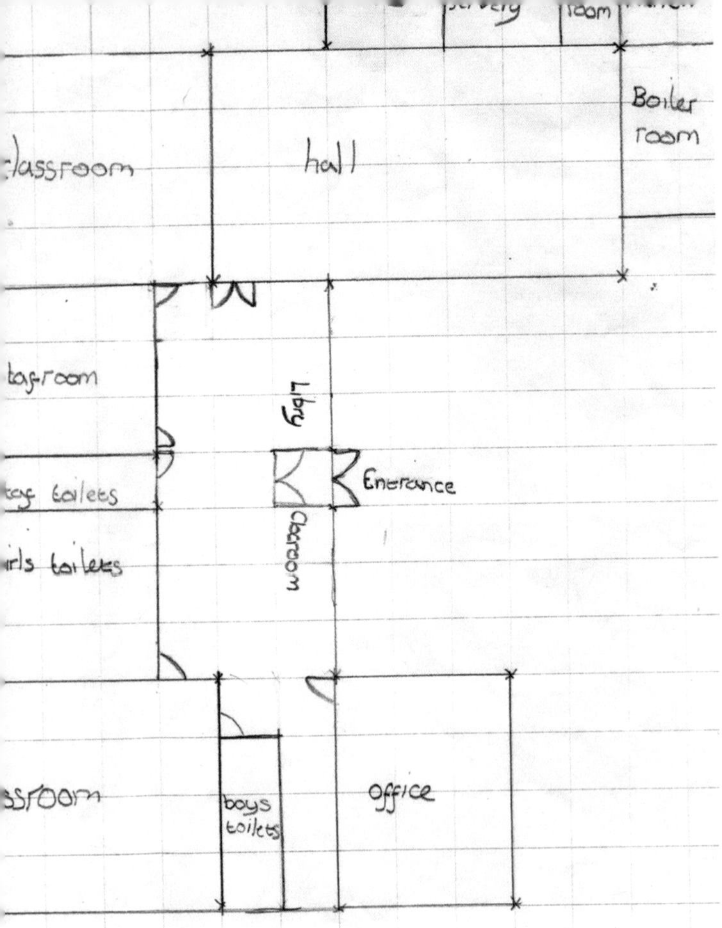

School today, by Denver Cheyne

The teaching staff (June 2012)

Una Ogg (infant teacher): There's such a wide variety of topics. We try to do things actively to interest the pupils, and do things in different ways so that it appeals to them in different ways. They're allowed to have a bigger say.

Julie Grant (classroom assistant): We've just got different ways o learning the children. Some of them learn better through practical, some of them learn better through writing, some kind o find that out, and we do our best to help them.

Una Ogg: I think in the country setting, things are slightly different; in many ways it may have disadvantages, but it's got many advantages as well, a nice setting here to do learning and do active things.

Julie Grant: Plus the staff aa works thegither, to help, so we're aa comin fae the same ...

Jane Mack: It's probably a more rounded education that they get [nowadays].

Una Ogg: There's a wide experience of art type things.

Jane Mack: And not so knowledge based, it's much more skills-based.

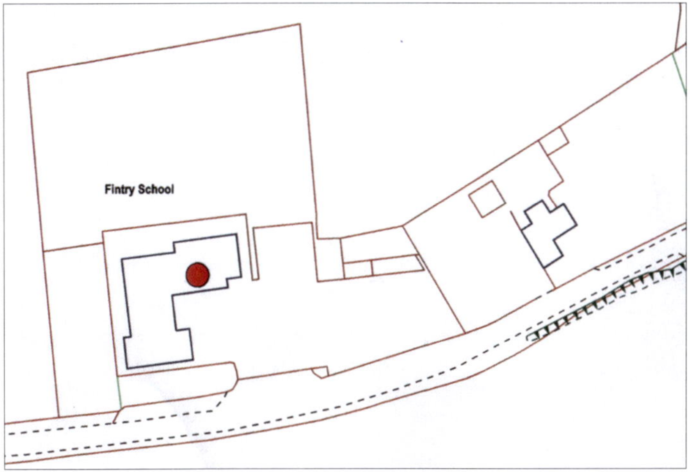

School plan, 2011 (COURTESY OF ABERDEENSHIRE COUNCIL)

Una Ogg: And a lot more group work, pair work,

Julie Grant: And of course there's [learning] support now, there never used to be support; that helps as well.

Jane Mack: There's a lot more children in mainstream education who wouldn't have been in mainstream education, even twenty years ago.

Una Ogg: In the last few years there's been hardly any training courses. Lately it's been more discuss things rather than some of the courses I've been on in the past which were so good and so helpful.

Hilary Anderson (learning support): The onus is far more on the individual person to support themselves really, and discover things themselves, rather than experts coming in.

Lorraine Hendry (head teacher relief): That's a token, sometimes, to do our Scottish poems, rather than have it totally integrated.

Una Ogg: But also in the curriculum, it is starting with your local community, finding out about local things, and then into Scotland, then higher up you're going more worldwide.

Julie Grant: I speak Scotch a lot.

Una Ogg: The only time I would do it if it's the time we were doing the poetry. The youngest ones, they come in, some of them are speaking quite broad. Sometimes it's quite appropriate, at other times if we're doing something the class has to understand, like a talking exercise, it might not be so appropriate. I'm flexible about it.

The Rainforest topic

Book launch

Una Ogg: We try to make all the activities fun, especially all the whole school things. We try to do quite a lot of whole school things and mix the groups.

Jane Mack: [We do] probably two or three whole school things every term, like the eco-party day, and they dress up.

Una Ogg: They dressed in green, they baked cakes, and they got to choose. They wanted shortbread, green icing. Some wanted a flag shape with green icing. We had cutters and did different shapes and put on green icing.

Jane Mack: Very green icing! And then, because it was such a nice day, we decided we'd do fun activities outside, so we hid various cards with bugs and flowers all around the school and they went in teams to find nine different bugs and flowers and identify them.

Una Ogg: We've done quite a bit of maths now, outside, we bought some new equipment for outside. They get sticks to count with or they get cubes and they've got to work in teams to find, to count in tens, or hundreds, or twos or fours, whatever it is.

Jane Mack: We're hoping to make the open bit of the shelter shed into a kind of outdoor classroom… so we can go out if it's a bit chilly, we've still got a bit of

Tree-planting, 2012, for the Diamond Jubilee

Former Pupils at the 180th Anniversary Open Day, 2011 – the Cruickshank sisters, Sheila, Ethel and Lilias

shelter. It's an initiative, from Aberdeenshire, well from the Scottish Government actually.

[For the Olympic Sports Day] we've bought medals, and we've got a rostrum, practised a dance for the opening ceremony, but basically sports will just be the normal races, which they get points for, and then we'll award a bronze, silver and gold medal. We're going to divide them into countries, and make flags, like an opening ceremony.

Lorraine Hendry: It's a very simple dance, and I had some help from the children as well. We just put in moves that we could find in Olympic sports, we put them together.

Jane Mack: I think the children do respect us.

Una Ogg: They'll come in in the morning and tell you things, they're desperate to tell you their news on news day. They tell you what they were doing at the weekend, things they've done at home, and if you've made something at school, they'll go home and try and make it. They talk a lot more to staff now.

Julie Grant: Some of our teachers were scary, you wouldna approach them. It's a lot more relaxed now. The school is the centre [of the community], we're aa approachable, and the parents ken they can approach us, and likewise.

Caroline Mackie (school administrator): It's a smaller school, friendlier.

Julie Grant: It's nae open-plan.

Hilary Anderson: It's not just the open plan. It's a very welcoming staff, a very welcoming school, the children

are nurtured here, as well as encouraged to take responsibility. It's a positive atmosphere, a positive ethos.

Caroline Mackie: It's a big family, actually. It's nice that you know the pupils from Primary 1 right to Primary 7. It's a real teamwork in school as well.

Janet Byth: Anything you dislike about your work here?

All: Paperwork! Laminating at the moment, laminate overload!

Parents and community comments

- My boy, who has autism, attended Fintry. Having a small number of people really helped him. All the teachers gave him extra support and understanding.
- My daughter loves it. Although the number of pupils has almost doubled there is still a lovely atmosphere.
- My son had a few problems but we had every help to overcome everything and he is a much happier boy now.
- [My son] lacked confidence, when he was in amongst big groups. He's getting a lot better now; Fintry School has done a lot for him, bringing him oot on himself.
- The difference between the old days, when the old school was there, if you wanted to get in to the hall, you simply went to the school house and a knock at the door, Miss Buchan came along, there's the key, but that's long since.
- There's a lot of new houses in the Fintry district, say within half a mile of the school. People are not necessarily working on the farms, they're working outside. They do their shopping elsewhere, they've all got cars, they all move out for their entertainment. Ease of transport makes people not get to know each other the same.
- There is a lot o Polish people. In the late eighties, a lot o English farmers came up, because farming was bad here at that time, and they had the money to come up and buy the farms. There's still a lot o English, they've aa moved out o the farms, they're staying in houses noo in different jobs. I ken the Fintry school was just kinda overrun with English a while.
- The bowling club, the judo, the badminton, and a these things that were held in the new community centre when the school was opened, they've all stopped. There's nothing like that now, the only thing the school's used for is maybe a meeting of some sort or our WRI meeting once a month.
- There's been a WRI at Fintry for more than eighty years. It's still going well, but in spite of the fact it was the community that contributed to that hall, we still have to pay quite a lot for the meetings. So we tend to have half our meetings in the school hall and half of

Community café, November 2014: Left to right, **standing adults:** Jane Mack (head teacher), Margaret Maxwell, Janet Byth, Ann Smith, Steve Smith, Val McManus, Alan Matthew holding AJ Matthew, Stella Duncan. **Pupils:** Evan Matthew, Elizabeth Maxwell, Angus McDonald, Madeleine Massey. **Seated:** Lynn Chambers, Lindsay Ledingham, Graeme Smith, Kirsteen Smith, Maryisa Mackenzie.

them outings to other places now. We still have a coffee morning, or a sale of work, to try and raise a bit of funds.

- I don't know if they were struggling for helpers or because the sports centre got built in Turriff. I think maybe some of the groups have gone there, and it just seems to be for the wider community.
- Fintry School is nae a cliquey school. Sometimes you can go to a bigger school, and there's five parents at one door, and whatever, I wouldna say Fintry's like that. Everyone speaks to everyone. But I dinna think they want to get in depth involved.

Primary 7 pupils look back

Sophie Mowatt: When I came to the school, I was a bittie nervous; there were other girls but I was the only one in Primary 1.

Sophie Clark: You get a lot of trips here. I really enjoy them, because they take you to lots of different places. We went to the Loch of Strathbeg, in Primary 2. And I wasn't looking where I was going and I fell into the loch. I had to sit on the bus soaking wet. And we've been to Haddo House, Fyvie Castle, and the theatre a couple of times.

Sophie Mowatt: We went bird watching [at the Loch of Strathbeg], and when we went into the bird watching bit, people were making noises so the birds flew away. And we went for a walk as well, around the forest, and we had our packed lunch outside on the benches.

Sophie Clark: The theatre - we went to see *Aladdin, Cinderella, Sleeping Beauty, Joseph and his Magic Coat.* I think it was His Majesty's in Aberdeen. There were about 20 schools there. One time we went to see [a show] and the bus broke down. And we couldn't get, we were all devastated. We had to wait about an hour and go straight home.

Aaron Weaver: My group [at Loch Insh], we did canoeing. That was very funny, one of the boats capsized, and they all got soaked.

Sophie Mowatt: We did raft building the night that we got there, and I did skiing. It was very jabby when you fell down on the dry ski slope.

Halloween party, 30 October 2011

Snakes and Ladders, 2011

Football pitch, 2011

Sophie Clark: My group, the guy telt us to push oor rafts and we had to run into the water and jump on to the rafts. There were two left standing and one of them fell to pieces in the water. They didn't tie the knots tight enough and the knots fell to pieces. And everyone fell right in.

Sophie Mowatt: Sometimes we had a picnic outside for lunch. Breakfast we had cereal and a cooked breakfast but you didn't need to have both if you didn't want to. You had your tea in the restaurant as well, there was only two things you could choose from, it was really good stuff, macaroni, and quiche, pizza, shepherd's pie.

Sophie Clark: You got apple and custard, and one night you got pancake and ice-cream. It was a very good camp to go to.

Sophie Mowatt: A happy life so far at this school. This school, they've taught you everything.

Sophie Clark: We got the flag for having a tidy, Eco School, like having the benches nice and painted, the pots nice and painted, the flowers nicely growing, and saving a lot of energy and water.

Aaron Weaver: We use the compost bin a lot, and grow tatties.

Sophie Mowatt: The Doctor Game – if you get caught, you have to put one arm behind your back, and if you get caught again, another arm, and if you get caught again, you have to hop, and if you get caught again you have to do five-star jumps, then you have to lie on the floor until there's a new game started again. If you were on the grass and it was wet you just crouch. If you're on the grass and it's really dry you lie down, and if you're on the tar, you just crouch down but you have to keep your arms and legs to yourself in case anyone stands on them or you trip someone up. It's a PE game, you'd never play it with the little ones, it's too dangerous.

Shark Attack - there's one shark but there's only a few islands [hoops are used] but if it's a small hoop you only get two people in or if it's a big hoop you get three people in. If there's too many in, one of them has to go out to get caught or find a new island, and if you get caught you have to be a shark until there's only one person left. Each round a hoop gets taken away, until there's only one or two hoops left.

Sophie Mowatt: We got them off Mrs Weaver; she made a book, a folder that had heaps of games in it. We didn't make up the games, they've already been invented; we just put them all into a book. We just started playing with them not that long ago, like the P7s before us, or the ones before them, they used to play them with us when we were little.

One person goes to the front, everyone else lines up further back and then the people that are lined up say, *'What's the Time, Mr Wolf?'* and the person that's the wolf would say *'Six o' clock'*. It doesn't matter which number he'd say, you'd have to take as much steps as he said, then they'd keep on saying till they'd got past the wolf. But if the wolf said *'Dinnertime'*, then he could catch people and they would be out.

Sophie Clark: The Animals Game, Crocodile River, there's crocodiles that side, and there's a hunter in the middle to catch them. They all have to join hands, and then catch them. You have to dodge them.

All the boys and girls [had lessons in skipping], then we did the show for the parents, we did the Double Dutch back skip, forward skip, crossovers, things like that, and at the end the parents had to go up and have a shot at skipping.

Sophie Mowatt: There was only a couple of people did Double Dutch. Mostly the P7s had to hold the big ropes when they were doing it because we're the oldest people and we have to help the other ones. We haven't continued the skipping lessons, but people do skip outside at playtime and lunchtime.

Aaron Weaver: We have done swimming lessons. We're the P7s and we've done everything. Other ones, like the P4s, they keep talking to us, when they should be really listening. They're the ones that have to learn it all.

African drumming was fun. You got these big drums, and he just gave you a beat and you had to try and play it.

Sophie Clark: And we made our own African drums and painted them, using tubs, but it had to be tubs that made a good beat. The music teacher, she did practising, and we had to copy. Making African drums was fun, but playing them was really fun as well.

Sophie Clark: Our topic last term was food from different countries. We had this food-tasting day, we tasted food from China, Mexico, India and Scotland, that was the four countries we were learning about.

The P7s all got this five paragraph [Scots poem] to learn called *Holiday Blues;* it was a really good one.

Sophie Mowatt: When I was in P4, we did about World War. We had to bring things in and put them in a timeline, a mug from 1960, wherever it went in the timeline. I took in my brother's slippers, and I took in a gasmask and something else from my granddad's house.

We went to see an author. Caroline Clough, she lives out of Turriff. And she showed us her book that she carries around, and puts down her notes. She gave us all a postcard with her signature on it. She'd written it all out by hand because every signature was a little bit different, all smudged and everything. She must have been really hard-working. She's a really good author, she's written two books altogether and she's working on a third.

Aaron Weaver: Yes, [we like playing football], except for the molehills. We have a tournament tomorrow, eight or nine schools, or seven or eight, coming and we're not so sure if we should have eight or seven players.

The coffee morning a couple of weeks ago - I found it fun. We were doing the sweetie stall and the lollipop stand. We didn't sell a lot of sweets but the lollipops, they went well.

Willow tunnel, 2011

Sophie Clark: Everyone wants to play with you on your last day, say goodbye, and at playtime, when you want to be by yourself, you could go to the hall. A few years ago, everyone went down to the hopscotch, and you could go down and give them a cuddle if you wanted to. I'll miss this school. It'll be hard to say goodbye.

Appendix 1:

Abstract of Subscription Lists and Disbursements Connected with the Building of Fintry School 1859-62

Charge By	£	s	d
Mr Pollard Urquhart, Esq., Craigston	15	0	0
Wm Morrison, Lower Cotburn	1	0	0
Geo. Wilson, Badentyre		15	0
Wm. Smith, Brackans	1	0	0
Troup, Bogs of Plaidy		17	6
Wm. Hay, Ferniestripe	1	0	0
Francis Souter, Banker		10	0
Geo. Lumsden, Towie Cottage	5	0	0
Alexander Gerrard, Bombay	1	0	0
John Ledingham	2	10	6
Collection at School	1	6	6
John Jesse, Esq., per J L	2	0	0
Rev A Mitchell		5	0
James Murray, Mill of Laithers	1	0	0
Robert Gerrard, London	1	0	0
John Rose, Turriff	1	0	0
John Robinson, Contractor		2	0
John Morrison, gamekeeper	1	0	0
Miss Morrison, Slackadale	1	0	0
Lecture and Soiree	7	19	10
Steele, Gardener, Craigston		5	0
Alexander Murray, Nethermill	1	1	0
James Wood, Midtown	5	0	0
Wood, Craig of Gairnieston		10	0
Wilson, Backhill		5	0
George Barclay, Yonderton	5	0	0
Wood, Moreless	1	0	0
Geo. Cowie, Newton		8	0
John Goldsman, Milton		7	6
W Morrison, Mill of Craigston		5	0
Mrs Ord, Mill of Craigston		1	6
Geo Morrison, Millseat		7	6
Barclay, North Mains		5	0
Louis Wilson, Blacksmith		7	6
John Smart, Carpenter		13	5
Rev William Findlay, King Edward	2	3	0
Mitchell, Balgreen	1	1	0

Mrs Paterson, late Midtown	7	0	0
Joass, Cowsmill	1	0	0
Al Ramsay, Banff		2	6
Mr Grant Duff, Esq. MP	1	0	0
Miss Morrison	2	0	0
Wm Morrison, Upper Cotburn	3	3	0
Pat Duncan, Balchers		3	6
Al Duncan, Land surveyor	1	1	0
Mrs Taylor, Mill of Balmaud	2	2	0
James Massie, Mason		2	6
John Minty, Shannocks, Elder		5	0
Alexr Adamson, Elder		5	0
Alexr Ledingham, Elder		5	0
Charles Wilson, Hilton, Elder		5	0
Francis Greig, Elder		5	0
John Thomson, Elder		5	0
Wm Smith, Brackans		10	0
James Wood, Midtown	1	0	0
Wm Morrison	1	0	0
John Sim		3	0
George Wilson		5	0

George C Morrison, Millseat	5	0
Miss Morrison	10	0
James Winton, Crossfields	2	0
Alexander Barber	1	0
William Sinclair	1	0
William Laird	2	0
John Paterson	1	0
Alexr Scorgie	1	0
Robert Hay	2	6
Monquhitter *per* Geo Wilson	5	0
Fraser, Kinbate	2	6
Robt Cruickshank, Bogs Laithers	2	6
John Murray	1	0
Peter Murray, Crossfields	5	0
John Ogg, Crossfields	1	0
John Watt, Crossfields		6
Mrs R McQueen	1	0
James Alexander, Rashes	3	0
Peter Gaul, Whiterashes	3	0
John Scott	2	0
Thomas Sharp		6

John Ledingham, Plaidy		1	0
James Wilson		2	0
Mrs Duncan, Back Plaidy		2	0
James Skene		1	0
George Thomson		2	6
John Robertson		2	0
Wm Duncan		3	0
James Hay, Ferniestripe		1	0
Murray & McCombie	2	2	0
James Duncan, Architect	5	5	0

Supplementary

Rev Wim Findlay		10	0
Mitchell, Balgreen	1	0	0
John Ledingham, Slap	1	0	0
Peter Cowie, Kinminty		10	0
Rev J Cruickshank, Turriff	1	0	0
A friend to Education	1	0	0
Mr Duncan, Fortrie	1	0	0
Robert Duncan, Banff		10	0
Alexr Mitchell, Balgreen		15	0
Joass, Cruichie		5	0
Miss M Mitchell		2	0
Concert by McLeod	3	10	0
Anderson, Cotwells		5	0
Wood, Craig		5	0
Jas Murray, Faichfolds		5	0
Reid, Boghead, Ord		2	6
John Grassie, Plaidy		3	0
Wm Hay, Ferniestripe		5	0
Mr Adamson, Writer, Banff		6	0
Morrison, Mains, Montcoffer		5	0
David Gill, Recloch		5	0
Robert Shand, Mains of Craigston		5	0
Louis Wilson, Blacksmith		3	0
G Barclay, North Mains		2	6
David Smart, Auchlin		5	0
Geo Cowie, Newton		5	0
Mrs Jamieson, Haughs		5	0
Adam Cruickshank, Millmoss		2	6
Patrick Duncan, Balchers		10	6
Mrs Duncan, Balchers		10	6

Wm Reid, Balchers		2	6
P Duncan, Milton Fishry		2	0
Rev John Milne, King Edward		5	0
A friend to Education		2	6
John Goldsman, Milton		4	0
Duff, Brownhill		2	6
Scott, Scatterty		5	0
Robert Walker, Montbletton		5	0
Use of school for lectures	1	0	0
Use of school Grant concert		5	0
Use of school McLeod concert		5	0
School holiday surplus Troup		14	0
Mr Geo Barclay a balance of 8/7		3	7
By interest on Cash in Bank		12	10
By Government Grant	123	0	0
Total Charge	**£240**	**4**	**8**

Discharge

James Massie, Mason	59	5	0
William Anderson, Slater	18	0	0
John Smart, Carpenter	67	11	05
John Gibson, Plasterer	9	0	0
Barry Henry & Co., Metal Standards	4	3	6
John Robinson, Excavator	6	10	0
Lovie & McQueen quarry and quarrying	27	4	1
Carriage of Lime Dallas		14	2
Al Murray, Valuator	1	1	0
Plan of site J L		10	6
Al Duncan, Land Surveyor	1	1	0
Advertisement Banffshire Journal		5	6
Feu Charter, Inglis & Leslie	16	19	7
Murray McCombie, Agents	9	1	11
Stationery and Postage	3	17	6
Jas Duncan, Architect	10	10	0
Interest to Union Bank	4	12	2
Total Discharge	**239**	**17**	**6**
Total Charge	240	4	8
Charge carried to account of school		**7**	**4**

Appendix 2:

Timeline of Fintry School

Year	National Education	Fintry School
1830		Site for Fintry school allocated by Earl of Fife.
1831		Foundation of Fintry School.
1839	Privy Council Committee on Education starts to award grants for maintenance of schools.	
1841		James Wilson, teacher living at Fintry Farm, noted in Census 1841.
1851		Hector Black, 'teacher of English', 33, in Fintry Schoolhouse, noted in Census 1851.
1859		Committee of Management formed 15 April, to fund and build new school.
1860		William Robb, died 13 December 1860, of consumption.
1861		William Hay, appointed 1861, resigned 28 March 1862 because of ill-health. New school building opened, date unknown.
1862		George Anderson, April 1862 - May 1866.
1866		John Arnott, July 1866 - August 1869.
1869		Alexander Stephen, Nov 1869 - Jan 1875
1872	Education (Scotland) Act	
1874		Fintry joins the new national system 4 March 1874
1875		George Andrew, Jan - Jun 1875; Henry Boyd appointed June 1875.

1877		Extra classroom added by extending northwards.
1878	School attendance becomes compulsory.	
1883		Henry Boyd suspended 5 February, tried and convicted 3 April, dismissed 8 May. Charles Shand, February 1883 - April 1886.
1886		John Brown, April 1886 - May 1887.
1887		James Elphinstone, May 1887 - April 1900.
1889	Fees abolished for elementary education.	
1891		Sixtieth anniversary of the school celebrated.
1892	County Committees on Secondary Education founded: Continuation Classes start for school leavers.	
1893		Third classroom added.
1900		James Clark, 1900 - September 1920.
1901	Supplementary Courses replace Specific Subjects: Leaving age raised to 14.	
1907		New schoolhouse built, old one becomes store.
1908	Education Act brings in medical inspections and other welfare measures.	
1918	Education (Scotland) Act 1918: end of School Boards, County Education Authorities set up.	
1920	Survey of educational provision in Aberdeenshire.	John Carrell, Nov 1920 – Nov 1923.
1923	Married women banned from teaching: Advanced Divisions replace Supplementary Courses.	Miss Mary Milne, interim October 1923 - April 1924.

1924	Promotion exams introduced, replacing 'qualifying' tests.	Miss Alice Corlett, April 1924 - May 1927; Miss Helen Buchan, May 1927 - June 1958.
1929	County Education Committees replace Education Authorities.	
1930	Report on post-qualifying education recommends keeping children as near home as possible, with common course in all schools.	Fintry designated a 'primary' school for future: 'Hot Dinners Scheme' inaugurated in December.
1937		Advanced Division pupils transferred to Turriff and King Edward secondary schools.
1939	Evacuation of children from large cities to country areas.	Fintry receives 35 evacuees.
1945	Education (Scotland) Act	
1946	Children's Act: Government Milk Scheme and School Meals introduced.	
1947	Scottish Council for Research in Education set up.	
1949		County School Meals start at Fintry.
1950	Memorandum on the Primary Curriculum.	
1953		Hall Committee set up to raise funds for building hall.
1958		Eric Taylor, August 1958 - July 1965.
1964		New school building opened 1 September.
1965	Memorandum on Primary Education in Scotland. Selection for secondary schooling abolished.	James Findlay, September 1965 - January 1971.

1971		Mrs Anne Sinclair (interim), January 1971 - June 1974.
1974	Teachers' Strike in December.	Mrs Catriona Tawse, August 1974 - June 1982.
1975	Regionalisation of Region's Advisory Service local government: and School Councils set up.	
1978	Warnock Report allows 'special needs' children to attend mainstream schools.	
1981	Parents' Charter gives right to choose school unless overcrowded: HMI's Teaching and Learning Report shows content and methods had remained traditional in spite of 1965 Memo.	
1982		Mrs Helen Findlay, August 1982 - June 1993.
1984	Abolition of corporal punishment in primary schools.	Spectrum computer bought for school use.
1987	*Curriculum and Assessment: a Policy for the 1990s* consultation paper introduces the 5-14 programme: National Testing resisted by teachers, parents and some authorities and abandoned in favour of testing by teachers as pupils moved through 5 -14 Programme.	
1989	Individual School Boards replace School Councils.	Election for Fintry School Board.
1993		Jan Filshie, August 1993 - June 2000.

1999	Scottish Parliament and Scottish Executive take control of Scottish education.	
2000		Laura Greig (Acting HT), Aug - Dec 2000.
2001		Louise Woolridge/Archibald, January 2001 - September 2004; [Peter Wood (maternity cover) Dec 2002 - May 2003].
2004	Curriculum for Excellence introduced, also Additional Support for Learning Act.	Jane Tedcastle (Acting HT), April 2004 - Dec 2004; Jane Tedcastle/Mack, December 2004 - present.

Appendix 3:

Account of Receipts and Expenditure in Connection with Schoolmaster's House and School Porch at Fintry, 1871–73

Receipts	£	s	d
Cash from subscriptions and as per list	63	11	10
Cash from Bank	94	0	0
	157	11	10
	155	7	5
	2	**4**	**5**

Acct. in connection with bazaar held at Turriff 6 August 1872

Free proceeds	125	16	1
Drawn from Bank	150	7	10
	278	8	4
	75	5	9
Balance in Mr Barclay's hand to pay carpenter	**2**	**19**	**0**

Expenditure

Jas. Barker for stones		7	6

John McDonald, mason, in full	27	17	6
Joseph Ross, plasterer, in full	17	18	0
John Reid for work		4	0
William Hepburn, slater, in full	15	1	10
James Barber for drains		5	6
Geddes & Co. for painting	2	15	0
Jn. Booker, carpenter, in full	64	11	0
John Smart for seal (?)		7	8
	155	**7**	**5**

Expenditure

Paid to Bank a/c	78	2	8
Paid discount on bill for £80	1	17	4
Renewal	1	5	9
Lamps to school	1	2	6
John McDonald, mason, for porch in full	16	19	6
Wm Hepburn, slater, to a/c (19s. to pay)	3	0	0
Jn. Booker, carpenter, to a/c (£2. 2s. to pay)	15	0	0
James Barber, putting in sewage pipes	1	12	9
Sewage pipes	2	6	6
Stones and branders for do.		10	9
Joseph Ross, plasterer, in full	1	14	6
Smith of Slap for railing and gate	4	11	6
Cook for painting	1	0	0
Bank bill & interest	80	4	9
Bank	13	0	10
Bank £5, £43	48	0	0
Mr. Duncan, architect	5	0	0
	275	**9**	**4**

Appendix 4:
HMI Report 1896

The structural arrangement of this school is not good. The junior room is too small for the number still taught in it, even though the second standard has been transferred to the senior room under the charge of a pupil teacher. There is no proper desk accommodation for them and they hamper the movements of the advanced scholars. The classroom recently built is small and it is filled to its utmost capacity by the pupils of the third and fourth standards. It is therefore very desirous that the junior room or the classroom should be extended so as to permit of a better arrangement of classes than that which at present prevails.

A globe for the proper teaching of geography should form part of the school equipment and suitable apparatus for drill including a piano should also be provided if full benefit is to be derived from the training given in this direction.

The work done must again be spoken of in terms of unstinted praise. The instruction given in the infant division is narrov in scope and could easily be broadened by the addition of some form of Kindergarten, and by giving a more prominent space to object lessons, but within the lines professed good results are shown. The second standard is week in Arithmetic but does well in every other respect while the third and fourth make an excellent appearance all round. Reading might be more expressive among the older pupils but despite this the general outcome of the teaching in the elementary subjects is so extremely satisfactory that the highest grant under Article 19B1(b) has been recommended. The answering in class subjects is good and all through the elementary science has been successfully taught. There is not even a tolerable approach to accuracy in the pronounciation of French, but in other respects the teaching has been very accurate. The training given in Latin has been most thorough. Very good singing, but a readier response to the ear tests is desirable. Sewing deserves very favourable notice. A grant under Article 19E is paid in respect of JT McBain but she should attend to Geography, Needlework and Music.

The pass in Agriculture of the scholar numbered 3 on Examination Schedule is disallowed under Article 21(e).

Merit Certificates are herewith enclosed for Ab.

Morrison, Jas. Burnett, Jas. Murray, Jessie Murray, A. Smith, An. Morrison and S. Barclay.

Merit Certificates cannot be granted to scholars under 13 years of age (Article 29).

Amount of grant earned . .	**£132**	**19s**	**6d**
4s overpaid		**4s**	
Amt. paid	**£132**	**15s**	**6d**

Average attendance **122**

Staff: **James Elphinstone MA (2nd class)**
WJ Paterson, ex-Pupil Teacher
Helen Chapman, ex-Pupil Teacher

Signed: **William F Stewart, Correspondent.**

Appendix 5:

HMI Report 1950-1

Report on Fintry visited 22 November 1950:

The roll has been fairly steady in recent years and on the day of inspection stood at 44. Attendance has been regular. With the exception of the floors, which were in some places rather uneven, the premises are in satisfactory condition. Redecoration had been carried out in 1949, and the provision of modern furniture and a new blackboard had greatly improved the head-teacher's classroom; it is desirable that, in the lower classroom also, the old-fashioned desks should be replaced by more modern ones. The playground had been recently resurfaced.

About 33 school meals, supplied daily from the kitchen at Crudie, are served in a spare room. The pupils listen regularly to various broadcast lessons. There is no cine-projector, but the teachers have displayed a large number of pictorial illustrations on the classroom walls, and the observation of nature at first hand is encouraged.

The probationer in charge of the three youngest classes was performing her task with vigour and with a considerable measure of success. She was making a creditable effort to ensure fluency in reading from the pupils at the PI (Infant) stage. All except one had a good knowledge of number. The pupils of class PII (Infant) read commendably well, and were able to add and subtract accurately. Only two of the pupils in class PIII, however, could read satisfactorily; the others were finding difficulty with phrasing. Proficiency in arithmetic at this stage was only passable. All three classes would benefit from regular oral training in answering questions clearly. Due attention had been given to the recreative subjects: in particular the three classes sang together very pleasantly.

In the other classroom there was an atmosphere of quiet purposeful endeavour, and the pupils were clearly interested in their work. Two girls in PIV read intelligently, but hesitancy marred the reading of the others. Oral answering to questions on the reading lesson was ready enough, and results in a test in arithmetic were fairly good. Class PV, however, did not appear to have a secure grasp of the arithmetic covered: it would be advisable to slacken the pace, at least for the weaker pupils. Attainment in class PVI was generally satisfactory. The pupils of class PVII made a favourable impression in all the subjects tested: their oral answers were commendably intelligent and, as a rule, well worded. Knowledge of spelling would be improved at all stages if a less ambitious choice of words were made. In every class the pupils had carefully memorised poems which they recited with praiseworthy expression. They also sang tunefully.

Adequate time had been devoted to art and handwork in the three youngest classes. Much credit is due to the teacher of the older pupils for the success attained in the studies of natural forms and in pattern-making; form, tone and colour were rendered with considerable skill.

In needlework, preparation had been undertaken with care. The girls of classes PVI and VII showed good manipulation in both knitting and needlework, but in the knitting of classes PIV and PV more attention should be paid to shaping.

Appendix 6:

Tenders Accepted for New School

JANUARY 1963	£	s	d
Mason work			
A J Chalmers & Son, New Pitsligo	10,625	18	0
Joiner work			
Garden & Watt, Turriff	4,342	1	4
Steelwork			
Hamilton Bros., Buckie	556	11	0
Metal Windows			
Standard McLean, Aberdeen	795	7	10
Slater and roughcast work			
W J C Eddie, Fyvie	943	15	4
Plumber work			
C McDonald & Sons, Turriff	1,589	15	0
Plaster work			
A D Walker, Banff	1,215	8	9
Floor finishes			
J N Stewart & Son, Aberdeen	304	12	0
Electrical work			
Turriff Electric, Turriff	846	1	6
Heating work			
G N Haden & Sons, Ltd., Aberdeen	1,845	13	1
Painter and Glazier work			
A Cumming, Turriff	1,010	10	0
	£24,075	**13**	**10**

Borrowing sanction sought for sum of £21,308 18 10, made up as follows:

		£	s	d
Total of tenders recommended for acceptance		24,075	13	10
Water rate (5s per £100 or part thereof)		60	5	0
Furniture and equipment:				
School Meals £82 5s 9d				
Others £887 10s 0d		969	15	9
		£25,105	**14**	**7**
LESS:				
(1) 100% School Meals Premises Grant				
Erection etc.	£1,942 0s 0d			
Furniture and equipment	£82 5s 9d			
	£2,024 5s 9d			
(2) Local Committee contribution				
	£1,762 10s 0d	3,786	15	9
		£21,318	**18**	**10**

Bibliography

Alexander Simpson, *Parish of Turriff, Old Statistical Account,* County of Aberdeen 1794

Alexander Simpson, *Parish of King Edward, Old Statistical Account,* County of Aberdeen 1794

James Cruickshank, *Parish of Turriff, New Statistical Account,* County of Aberdeen 1842

William Findlay, *Parish of King Edward, New Statistical Account,* County of Aberdeen 1840

Census Returns 1841-1901

Accounts of King Edward Kirk Session, CH2/114/17 (National Archives of Scotland)

The War Book of Turriff and Twelve Miles Round, ed. J Minto Robertson (Turriff and District Ex-Servicemen's Association, 1926)

Fintry School Committee of Management, Minutes and Abstract of Accounts 1859-1873 (in private ownership)

Annual Grants Form No IV, ED/18, October 1862 (National Archives of Scotland)

Fintry School Log Book, 3 vols, 1864-1994; Grampian Region Education Dept., Banff/Buchan Division (Aberdeen City Archives)

Minutes of Turriff School Board, vols 3-5, 1884-1994 (Aberdeen City Archives)

Crown Office Precognitions against Henry Boyd 1883, AD14/83/263 (National Archives of Scotland)

Education Authority: County of Aberdeen, Minutes, 11 vols, 1919-1930 (Aberdeen City Archives)

Education Committee, County of Aberdeen, Minutes, 11 vols, 1930-1975 (Aberdeen Central Library)

Fintry Hot Dinner Scheme Minutes (in private ownership)

Fintry School Admission Register 1936-71, (Aberdeen City Archives)

Grampian Regional Council Education Committee Minutes (Aberdeen Central Library)

The Primary School in Scotland: SED Edinburgh, HMSO, 1950: a Memorandum on the Curriculum

Primary Education in Scotland: SED Edinburgh, HMSO, 1965: The Primary Memorandum
Kent Road Junior Secondary School No. 705, Log Book D-ED7/116/1/4 (Glasgow Mitchell Library)
Kent Road Admissions Register, Boys, D-ED7/10/1-2, and Girls, D-ED7/11/2-4 (Glasgow Mitchell Library)
Aberdeen Journal, April 1883
Banffshire Journal 1845-present
Turriff Advertiser 1937-present